THE BEDFORD SERIES IN HISTORY AND CULTURE

The Saint Bartholomew's Day Massacre

A Brief History with Documents

Related Titles in
THE BEDFORD SERIES IN HISTORY AND CULTURE
Advisory Editors: Lynn Hunt, *University of California, Los Angeles*
David W. Blight, *Yale University*
Bonnie G. Smith, *Rutgers University*
Natalie Zemon Davis, *Princeton University*
Ernest R. May, *Harvard University*

THE BEDFORD SERIES IN HISTORY AND CULTURE

The Saint Bartholomew's Day Massacre

A Brief History with Documents

Barbara B. Diefendorf

Boston University

BEDFORD/ST. MARTIN'S   Boston ◆ New York

For Natalie Zemon Davis

For Bedford/St. Martin's

Publisher for History: Mary V. Dougherty
Director of Development for History: Jane Knetzger
Senior Editor: Heidi L. Hood
Developmental Editor: Louise Townsend
Editorial Assistant: Katherine Flynn
Production Supervisor: Andrew Ensor
Production Associate: Samuel Jones
Executive Marketing Manager: Jenna Bookin Barry
Text Design: Claire Seng-Niemoeller
Project Management: Books By Design, Inc.
Index: Books By Design, Inc.
Cover Design: Joy Lin
Cover Art: *St. Bartholomew's Day Massacre, 24 August 1572* (oil on panel) by François
    Dubois (1529–1584). Musée Cantonal des Beaux-Arts de Lausanne, Switzerland.
    Photo © Held Collection/The Bridgeman Art Library.
Composition: TexTech International
Printing and Binding: RR Donnelley & Sons Company

President: Joan E. Feinberg
Editorial Director: Denise B. Wydra
Director of Marketing: Karen R. Soeltz
Director of Editing, Design, and Production: Marcia Cohen
Assistant Director of Editing, Design, and Production: Elise S. Kaiser
Manager, Publishing Services: Emily Berleth

Library of Congress Control Number: 2008923368

Manufactured in the United States of America.

3 2 1 0 9 8
f e d c b a

For information, write: Bedford/St. Martin's, 75 Arlington Street, Boston, MA 02116
(617-399-4000)

ISBN-10: 0-312-41360-2
ISBN-13: 978-0-312-41360-6

Acknowledgments
Acknowledgments and copyrights appear at the back of the book on page 166, which
constitutes an extension of the copyright page.

Distributed outside North America by PALGRAVE MACMILLAN.

Foreword

The Bedford Series in History and Culture is designed so that readers can study the past as historians do.

The historian's first task is finding the evidence. Documents, letters, memoirs, interviews, pictures, movies, novels, or poems can provide facts and clues. Then the historian questions and compares the sources. There is more to do than in a courtroom, for hearsay evidence is welcome, and the historian is usually looking for answers beyond act and motive. Different views of an event may be as important as a single verdict. How a story is told may yield as much information as what it says.

Along the way the historian seeks help from other historians and perhaps from specialists in other disciplines. Finally, it is time to write, to decide on an interpretation and how to arrange the evidence for readers.

Each book in this series contains an important historical document or group of documents, each document a witness from the past and open to interpretation in different ways. The documents are combined with some element of historical narrative—an introduction or a biographical essay, for example—that provides students with an analysis of the primary source material and important background information about the world in which it was produced.

Each book in the series focuses on a specific topic within a specific historical period. Each provides a basis for lively thought and discussion about several aspects of the topic and the historian's role. Each is short enough (and inexpensive enough) to be a reasonable one-week assignment in a college course. Whether as classroom or personal reading, each book in the series provides firsthand experience of the challenge— and fun—of discovering, recreating, and interpreting the past.

Lynn Hunt
David W. Blight
Bonnie G. Smith
Natalie Zemon Davis
Ernest R. May

Preface

The most notorious episode in sixteenth-century Europe's civil and religious wars, the events known collectively as the "Saint Bartholomew's Day Massacre" are of lasting historical importance. The murder of thousands of unarmed French Protestants by Catholic soldiers and civilians in August 1572 influenced not only the subsequent course of France's civil wars but also, more broadly, the process of French state building, patterns of international alliance, and long-term cultural values. To such Enlightenment writers as Montesquieu and Voltaire, the killings epitomized the horrors of fanaticism and unexamined belief, and it seems natural to see the massacre in those terms today. In the immediate aftermath of these events, however, they were viewed very differently. Protestants reacted with horror, but Catholic leaders at home and abroad congratulated the young king, Charles IX, who publicly claimed credit for destroying his Protestant enemies and had medals struck to celebrate his triumph. Charles's image of a just and valiant king later gave way to its opposite, and in histories, novels, and films, he has been depicted either as a treacherous tyrant who conspired to murder his own subjects or as the unwitting tool of his scheming mother. Whatever the truth of the matter, the Saint Bartholomew's Day Massacre raises troubling questions about the relationship between religion and politics, the moral responsibility of secular and religious authorities, and the origins and consequences of religious persecution and intolerance. These problems remain acutely important in the world today.

The breadth and depth of the massacre's repercussions, but also perplexing questions of responsibility for these events, make the Saint Bartholomew's Day Massacre an ideal subject for study and debate. The introduction and documents in this volume give a broad view of the social, political, and religious origins of the massacre, the complex events that unfolded in Paris and the provinces, and the longer-term repercussions of these events. They enable students to explore the roots of some of the key transitions from the medieval to the modern world, including the passage from divine-right monarchy to social-contract theories of government, from a unified faith to religious pluralism, and from the persecution of religious dissidents as threats to the social order to toleration and the separation of church and state. At the same time, they allow students to examine the causes and consequences of perhaps the most disturbing episode of civil and religious conflict during this troubled era.

The introduction in part one provides an overview of the political and religious context in which the massacre occurred. Describing the origins and spread of Protestant ideas in France, it explains why Catholics found them so threatening and narrates the collision between growing religious tensions and political factionalism that resulted in a series of civil wars beginning in 1562. After locating the more distant roots of the Saint Bartholomew's Day Massacre in these conflicts, it summarily traces the course of the massacre in Paris and the provinces and outlines its immediate and long-term repercussions, both domestically and internationally. The documents in part two include such official records as royal edicts and magistrates' reports but also firsthand accounts, after-the-fact polemics and commentary, visual sources, poetry, and song. Most of the written sources have never before been translated into English and appear here for the first time. Arranged chronologically, they permit students to analyze the evolving political and religious conflicts and their outcomes from a variety of points of view. Headnotes identify each document's author and provide historical context. Additional learning aids in this volume include footnotes identifying unfamiliar terms and concepts, a list of major figures, genealogical charts for the royal family and key aristocrats, and an appendix containing a chronology of the French Wars of Religion, questions for consideration, and a selected bibliography.

ACKNOWLEDGMENTS

This book has benefited greatly from the comments, suggestions, and encouragement I have been given along the way. I thank Lynn Hunt for first suggesting the idea of a documentary history of the Saint Bartholomew's Day Massacre. My thanks to another editor of the Bedford Series in History and Culture go even farther back. Natalie Davis introduced me to the massacre as a graduate student but also taught me how to read and think about sixteenth-century source materials. This book is dedicated to her. Sincere thanks to Megan Armstrong, McMaster University; Michael Breen, Reed College; Gayle K. Brunelle, California State University Fullerton; Mack Holt, George Mason University; Howard Louthan, University of Florida; and William Patch, Washington & Lee University. Your careful reading of the manuscript and thoughtful questions have prompted many revisions. Thanks also to the students who have tried out these documents in several different classes over the years. Your comments too have helped to focus this volume. I am grateful to the many early modernist friends who have encouraged the project by telling me to hurry and finish so they can use the book in their classes. I appreciate your confidence. I appreciate also the support and patience shown by Jane Knetzger and Mary Dougherty at Bedford/St. Martin's and the assistance of Shannon Hunt and Katherine Flynn at various stages in the project. My editor, Louise Townsend, did a superb job of helping me to pare down and refine the manuscript, and Emily Berleth and Nancy Benjamin skillfully saw it through to publication. Last, but certainly not least, Jeffry Diefendorf has read, reread, and lived with this manuscript with more patience than anyone has a right to expect.

Barbara B. Diefendorf

A Note about the Text and Translation

Most of the documents included here have never been translated into English, and all translations except where noted are my own. All translation requires a balancing act; the texts included here are no exception. I have tried to keep the texts as accurate as possible but at the same time to render them into readable English with undergraduate readers in mind. Sixteenth-century French is stylistically very different from the English we use today. Phrasing was often long and convoluted, with multiple subordinate clauses, double-barreled modifiers, and punctuation that followed no set rules. To make the texts more readable, I have sometimes had to break up and rearrange sentences, and the translations are in general somewhat freer than they would be for a work aimed at a scholarly audience. At the same time, I have tried where possible to limit these interventions so as to preserve something of the flavor of the original as well as the integrity of its patterns of speech and thought.

Contents

PART TWO

The Documents   **39**

APPENDIXES

Maps and Illustrations

PART ONE

Introduction: Saint Bartholomew's Day and the Problem of Religious Violence

Early on the morning of August 24, 1572 (Saint Bartholomew's Day by the church calendar), Catholic troops began to slaughter unarmed Protestants who had gathered in Paris for a royal wedding. These actions led to a wave of popular violence that resulted in the deaths of an estimated two thousand to three thousand men, women, and children. Contemporary observers recount atrocious scenes of brutality. According to one often reproduced early account, "The streets were covered with dead bodies; the river tinted with blood; and the doors and gates to the king's palace painted the same color" (Document 22). The killing subsequently spread to other French towns in waves that left as many as five thousand to six thousand people dead. These figures are not large when compared with the twentieth century's horrific episodes of mass murder, and yet they remain profoundly disturbing. Why did anyone need to die for their religious beliefs in sixteenth-century France? Why did religious differences introduced by the Protestant Reformation result not just in official persecution but also in popular religious animosities strong enough to provoke the slaughter of neighbor by neighbor? Why did the king, who claimed to be the protector and father of his people, take credit for ordering the killings? And why do these events still have such historical resonance that the pope was forced to address lingering resentments when he said Mass in Paris exactly 425 years later?

The Saint Bartholomew's Day Massacre poses challenging questions about historical causation, responsibility, and meaning. There were no impartial observers. All of the accounts we have of these events—and there are many—are consciously or unconsciously slanted so as to frame the actions of various participants in particular ways. This was done to cast blame on certain individuals and exonerate others, but it was also done to manipulate perceptions of the fundamental motives behind the massacre, which was presented on the one hand as the necessary response to an impending coup and on the other hand as premeditated and unprovoked murder. If the former interpretation aimed to justify the slaughter, the latter aimed to justify the Protestant revolt that occurred in its wake. It is necessary to read conflicting accounts of the massacre critically and to realize that the authors' interpretive biases influenced not only the ways they depicted the principal parties involved in these events but also the ways they represented popular participation in the killing, the role of both local authorities and the aristocratic clans competing for power at court, and the international ramifications of the massacre. The primary sources surrounding the Saint Bartholomew's Day Massacre thus raise broad questions about religious violence and the domestic and international repercussions of religious persecution, but they also raise more specific questions about the relative responsibility of the king and his advisers, the governing elites, and the French populace for a complex chain of rapidly unfolding events.

To address these questions properly, we need first to examine the role that religion played in late medieval society and the changes introduced by the Protestant Reformation. We will then look at the buildup of religious tensions in France, the outbreak of civil war, and the events that led up to the massacre. Because there are no impartial sources, we will examine the murders that took place in Paris and various provincial cities through a variety of Protestant and Catholic accounts and then look more closely at the repercussions of the massacre in France and abroad.

(Opposite)   Sixteenth-Century Paris

With a population of 250,000 to 300,000 people, sixteenth-century Paris was the largest city in northern Europe. The area enclosed by its walls nevertheless remained compact enough that one could walk around it in about three hours.

Bibliothèque nationale de France.

The Saint Bartholomew's Day Massacre may be the most infamous incident of confessional violence that occurred during the early modern period, but the tensions that exploded in the incident and even many of the acts of retributory violence that followed were far from unique. Religious riots and attacks on perceived heretics occurred in various parts of Europe when religious unity was shattered by the Protestant Reformation. Areas that largely escaped such overt conflicts—for example, Italy and Spain—did so because authorities there acted decisively to stifle any sign of dissent, not because either leaders or people were more tolerant of change. The Saint Bartholomew's Day Massacre thus offers an excellent laboratory for examining the impact of religious dissent and the formation of new confessional alignments on European culture and society. It also offers valuable insights into the profound social and political dislocation that occurred when rival churches staked competing claims to religious truth.

RELIGIOUS FAITH IN AN INSECURE WORLD

In the later Middle Ages, people lived precarious lives, vulnerable to disease, famine, and many other sources of hardship and early death. Religion provided the first line of defense against these vulnerabilities. It helped people to cope with the uncertainties of life by giving meaning to a world that often seemed chaotic, harsh, and unfair. It legitimated social hierarchies and political authority, facilitated social order by establishing codes of right and wrong, and offered hope to those struggling on the margins, who would get their reward in the life to come, if not here below.

The church sought to meet these challenges through both doctrine and ritual. The vast majority of people were poorly educated, if not totally illiterate, and had only a rudimentary understanding of church doctrine.[1] The church assured them, however, that by participating fully in its rituals, they could enjoy its benefits in this life and the next. Jesus died on the Cross to redeem the sins of the world, and priests reenacted Christ's sacrifice in the sacrament of the Eucharist every time they celebrated Mass. When the priest said the holy words of consecration over the bread and wine of the Eucharist, these elements were transformed into the body and blood of Christ, as Jesus had promised his disciples at the Last Supper. By witnessing the ritual of the Mass, Christians believed, they shared in the special grace, or blessings, with which God rewarded this repetition of Christ's sacrifice.

With God's grace, Christians were taught, they might lead good lives, doing good works and earning more grace, so that when they died, they would have their reward in heaven. They were taught that humans are frail and prone to sin; they would falter many times, despite their best intentions. The church offered a remedy for this in the sacrament of penance. By confessing one's sins to a priest and doing the penance he prescribed, the penitent sinner could receive absolution and set out once more on the path to heaven. People who did not confess their sins and receive absolution for them were condemned to work out their penalties in purgatory or—if guilty of serious, or "mortal," sins—condemned to the fires of hell forever.

If the church sought to offer people reassurance and the hope of reward, it also sought to keep them in line by the threat and fear of punishment. Both sides of the coin of religion—reassurance and fear—are evident in the later Middle Ages. Some historians have identified a kind of bookkeeping mentality—an arithmetic of salvation—in the attempts of late medieval clerics and laypeople to try to calculate just how much punishment various sins might entail. At the same time, the church attempted to ease the burden of penance by increasingly allowing people the option of substituting cash payments for acts of reparation, such as going on pilgrimage or reciting certain prayers. Martin Luther's challenge to this practice, known as the "sale of indulgences," began the Protestant Reformation and permanently divided Western Christendom.

THE ORIGINS AND SPREAD OF THE PROTESTANT REFORMATION

Luther did not intend to divide the church when he spoke against indulgences in 1517. He wanted only to reform a practice he thought harmful to the spiritual health of Christian believers, who might be tempted to think they could free themselves of the burden of sin by paying a fine instead of repenting in their soul. But the sale of indulgences was profitable to the church, which naturally fought back. So did Luther, whose theology became more radical as he sought to defend himself. Taking the Bible as his sole authority, Luther argued that all the indulgences people buy, all the ceremonies they witness, all the good works they do cannot get them into heaven. People are saved by faith, God's gift of grace, as revealed directly in scripture. This posed a direct threat to the church's theology of salvation and

also to the sacred character of the priesthood and the supreme authority of the pope in religious matters.

Such a challenge could not go unanswered. The pope condemned
Luther as a heretic, but because of the political situation in the Holy
Roman Empire, Luther escaped the traditional punishment of death by
burning and was allowed to live. Though forced into hiding, he wrote
prolifically. Treatises and polemics streamed from his pen and were
published, translated into other languages, and distributed across Europe. Meanwhile, a growing circle of followers sought to put Luther's
ideas into practice by restructuring religious services according to
this new theology. The same political turmoil that allowed Luther to
escape execution for heresy allowed these followers to begin to imple-
ment his ideas in the Holy Roman Empire, whose decentralized government permitted great opportunity for local initiative. By contrast, in
the more centralized kingdom of France, the monarchy was able if not
to eliminate Luther's ideas, at least to drive them underground.

The theology faculty at the University of Paris formally condemned
Luther's teachings in 1521. France burned its first "Lutheran" heretic
two years later. And yet the new ideas continued to spread, especially
among merchants with contacts abroad, skilled artisans, and university students and faculty. John Calvin was one of those student converts.
When persecution made France too dangerous for him and his friends,
they fled to safer places in Switzerland and the Holy Roman Empire.
Although Calvin still considered himself a neophyte in the new faith,
he was soon invited to take direction of the Reformation in progress
in Geneva, just across the border from France. Organizing the new
church, negotiating relations with secular authorities, and elaborating
a systematic Reformed theology took a lot of Calvin's energy during
the years that followed, but he never lost sight of a goal dear to his
heart: to convert his native France to the Reformed faith. He directed
special appeals to the high nobility in the hope that they might lead a
top-down reformation as some German princes had done. He also
trained ministers in Geneva and smuggled them back into France. As
a result, when French converts to the new ideas began to organize
clandestine churches in the 1550s, they tended to adopt Calvin's theology and the organizational structures of Geneva's Reformed church.

The printing press played a key role in disseminating the new ideas.
French printers risked their lives by secretly printing forbidden books.
So did booksellers who trafficked in the theological and polemical
works that began to be published in Geneva and smuggled into France.
Some of these polemics attacked the corruption and venality repre-

sented by the sale of indulgences and other Catholic practices; others offered instruction in Protestant ideas through derogatory comparisons with Catholic teachings (Document 1).

Protestants were not alone in wielding the weapon of polemic. Catholic propagandists denounced the new beliefs as heresy and derided those who adopted them as atheists who had abandoned God to follow their own perverse inclinations. They represented the new ideas as a war being waged against the City of God by its carnal enemies (Document 2) and recirculated stories that had first arisen in the early church associating heresy with debauchery. Although there was no foundation for the accusation that Protestants were sexual libertines, a great many French Catholics accepted the idea without question. When Protestants were arrested for attending clandestine religious services in a house in Paris's rue Saint-Jacques in 1557, Catholics gleefully circulated rumors that they had been caught practicing a "fraternal charity" that was sexual in nature, offering "their belongings and bodies to those who wished to follow them" (Document 3).

A report from the Reformed church of Paris asking Protestant leaders in Switzerland to intervene with the king on their behalf tells a very different story of the affair of the rue Saint-Jacques and of the church's history and practices (Document 4). As the report indicates, the church had been founded only two years prior to the affair. Like other French Reformed churches, it was founded when Protestant converts, tired of participating in Catholic rituals in which they no longer believed, decided to create the institutional structures that would allow them to worship according to their beliefs. To do so entailed new risks, because the authorities judged participation in the Protestant sacraments of baptism and Communion a more serious crime than listening to heretical sermons or reading forbidden books.

Reformed church members accepted these risks because they accepted Calvin's refusal to separate inward belief from the outward manifestations of this belief. In a number of influential treatises and sermons, Calvin railed against those who sought to avoid persecution by outwardly continuing Catholic practices while secretly subscribing to the new ideas. Joining the concept of sanctification to Luther's notion of justification by faith, Calvin insisted that true faith made itself known only in the process of living out one's beliefs. Faced with persecution, the faithful had just two choices: They could flee to a place where they could practice their religion freely, or they could accept the prospect of persecution and steel themselves for martyrdom. In all, approximately 450 men and women were executed for heresy in sixteenth-century France.[2] To the believing French Protestant, the danger of suffering a public and horrifying death seemed very real (Documents 5 and 6).

The threat of persecution had a profound effect on the character of the French Reformed church. While it enlarged the flow of refugees to Geneva and other Swiss and German towns, it also helped forge a militant church, whose members celebrated courage and constancy and prepared, if necessary, to suffer for their faith. Accounts of Protestant conversions consistently distinguish between an individual's first introduction and attraction to the new ideas and the crucial moment, which often occurred during illness or at a time of extreme stress, when that individual resolved to accept the Reformed faith regardless of the consequences (Document 7).

Despite the risks, the new ideas were spreading rapidly by the late 1550s. Within a few years, as many as twelve hundred Reformed churches had been established in France. The social geography and sociology of Protestant conversion were complex; local conditions and traditions strongly influenced receptivity to the new faith. A few generalizations can, however, be hazarded. Conversion efforts were most successful in the south of France, where a great number of Reformed churches were established in a broad arc that stretched from Poitou in the west through Guyenne and Languedoc into the Rhône Valley and Dauphiné. The efforts that Calvin and other church leaders made to convert the French aristocracy knew their greatest success in this area, and these aristocrats in turn offered patronage and protection to newly established churches. By contrast, conversion efforts were far less successful across a parallel but more northerly arc that ran from Brittany in the west through the central highlands and across Burgundy and Champagne, both because of resistance from powerful noble leaders and because of the depth with which Catholic loyalties were ingrained on the popular level.

In general, moreover, conversion efforts succeeded best among more literate and highly skilled urban populations. Few peasants or manual laborers adopted the new faith, and artisans engaged in newer and more skilled crafts converted more often than those working in traditional or lower-status trades. Prosperous merchants and members of the liberal professions also converted in disproportionate numbers; it seems that the Protestant emphasis on personal faith resonated with the sense of self-worth of these upwardly mobile urban groups. For the same reason, Protestantism exerted a strong initial attraction for magistrates and royal officers. Most, however, backed away quickly when

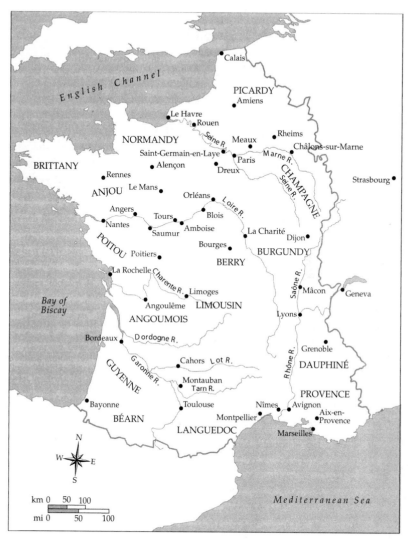

France during the Wars of Religion

the crown's condemnation of heresy forced them to choose between their new religious inclinations and the advantages they enjoyed as royal officials. A notable exception was Anne du Bourg, a magistrate in the Parlement of Paris, who was burned at the stake for his beliefs in 1559 (Document 6).

As a percentage of the French population, the aggregate number of Protestant converts always remained small—at most 10 to 15 percent—and yet the disproportionate attraction the new religion held for the most articulate and prosperous members of the middle classes, as well as the large number of noble converts, made the new religion appear far more threatening than numbers alone might suggest. Or so it seemed to France's king, Henry II, when he put an end to a long series of foreign wars by negotiating peace with Spain in 1559 and returned home intending to stop the spread of heresy. As it happened, Henry was unable to pursue this objective. A jousting accident at the festivities intended to celebrate the peace cost the king his life. The same fatal accident let loose factional rivalries at court that only Henry's firm hand had kept in check. His widow, Catherine de Medici, struggled to maintain control for her young sons as an ardently Catholic faction headed by the Guise family, a younger branch of the house of Lorraine, fought to dominate policymaking in opposition to a Protestant-leaning faction headed by members of the house of Bourbon, who were princes of royal blood.

Francis, duke of Guise, and his brother Charles, cardinal of Lorraine, had an initial advantage in the rivalry. Uncles by marriage to the new

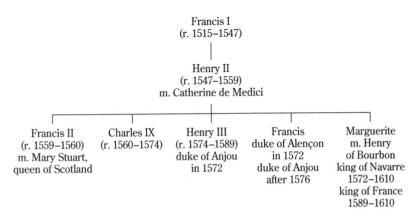

Family Tree for the Later Valois

king, Francis II, they became his principal advisers and persuaded him to increase persecution of religious dissidents. Protestants responded by plotting to seize the young king at his Loire Valley castle of Amboise and free him from "the tyrants' yoke," but word of the plan leaked out, and it was the conspirators who were seized instead. Several hundred Protestant noblemen were captured and hanged from a railing at Amboise as a warning to others who might contemplate rebellion. Only the unexpected death of Francis II in December 1560 saved the Protestant leader, Louis of Bourbon, prince of Condé, from being executed for conspiracy as well.

The tumult of Amboise damaged the Protestant cause by associating adherents to the new faith with political rebellion against the crown. Francis II's death nevertheless brought about a change in royal policy that was favorable to the Huguenots, as the Protestants now began to be called.[3] Queen Mother Catherine de Medici assumed the powers of regent and governed in the name of her eleven-year-old son, Charles IX. Attempting to maintain peace in the troubled kingdom, she moderated the Guises' policy of persecution and issued an edict in April 1561 that forbade injuring anyone on account of his or her private religious beliefs. Unfortunately, the plan to ease tensions through the new policy of limited toleration miscarried. Catherine had misjudged not only the growing popularity of the new religion and the boldness of its leaders but also the level of popular animosity directed against it.

Although the edict of April 1561 explicitly forbade Protestants to worship in public, they continued to gather in increasingly large numbers for sermons and prayer. They also began to seize churches in the cities where they were strongest and to engage in acts of iconoclasm, deliberately destroying saints' images and other ritual objects so as to publicize alleged errors in Catholic teaching. A provisional edict issued in July 1561 attempted to put a stop to this behavior but had little effect. Meanwhile, the Catholic majority, egged on by zealous preachers who compared heresy to a cancer or gangrene that had to be cut out to restore the health of the social body, was becoming increasingly angry. Incidents of religious violence multiplied, as Catholic crowds attacked Huguenots returning from worship and set fire to buildings where they were known to gather (Document 8).

In Paris, tensions rose to new heights in December 1561, when Protestants worshipping in a house in the faubourg[4] of Saint-Marcel clashed with Catholics attending Mass in the neighboring church of Saint-Médard. The battle started when Protestants, whose services

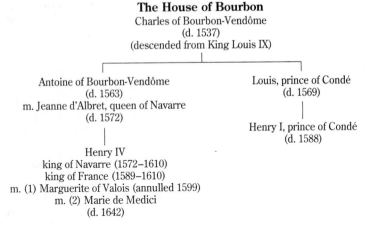

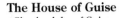

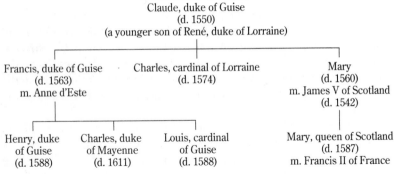

Family Trees for the Houses of Bourbon and Guise

had been disturbed by Saint-Médard's tolling bells, sent a delegation to ask that the bells be silenced. Accounts of what happened next differ. Catholics claimed that the Huguenots, "without other provocation, ran to sack this poor church." They attacked priests, broke the heads off saints' statues, and ground the consecrated host under their feet (Document 9). Protestants countered by insisting that the Catholics had begun the violence by murdering one of the envoys sent to ask for the bells to cease (Document 10). The riot remained a sore point for Catholics, moreover, because it appeared that the officials sent to restore order had sided with the Protestants, whose assembly, in the Catholics' opinion, should never have been permitted in the first place. From the Protestants' point of view, the Catholics more than took their revenge the next day when they set fire to one of the buildings where the Huguenots held their services.

A few weeks later, Catherine tried again to calm the situation by issuing a compromise edict in the king's name. The edict of January 1562 ordered Protestants to return churches and properties seized from Catholics. It also repeated earlier injunctions against holding religious services within city limits, going to services in arms, and speaking abusively of Catholic doctrine or ceremonies. For the first time, however, it permitted Protestants to gather legally for prayer and sermons, as long as these services took place outside city walls. It also offered them some protection by explicitly forbidding Catholics to disturb them as they went to services and ordering magistrates to enforce this law.

Once again, however, Catherine's attempt at compromise offended people on both sides of the religious divide. Protestants complained that their right to worship was still too limited, while Catholics were outraged that any worship was permitted at all. Still angry over the Saint-Médard affair, Catholic Parisians were especially outspoken in their opposition to the new edict. The Parlement of Paris refused to register it as law until twice ordered to do so by the king. The theologians of the Sorbonne,[5] a delegation of French clergy, the Paris City Council, and other groups protested as well, all without success.

Given the level of anger in the city, it is not surprising that when, two months later, troops commanded by Francis, duke of Guise, attacked Protestants gathered for worship at Vassy, near a Guise estate in Champagne, many Parisians acclaimed him as their hero. Here, people believed, was the Catholic leader who would put an end to the Huguenots' insolence. When he arrived in Paris, Guise was greeted with a public welcome usually reserved for royalty. A large company of noble and bourgeois leaders came to meet him, while a cheering populace lined the streets. A popular song celebrating the duke's role at Vassy even began to circulate (Document 11).

The Massacre of Vassy put an end to Catherine's attempt to keep peace through a policy of limited toleration. When the duke of Guise refused to apologize for the deaths and injuries the incident had caused, Huguenot leader Louis of Bourbon, prince of Condé, withdrew from court, seized the town of Orléans, and prepared for war. France's religious conflicts had reached the stage where they could be settled only on the battlefield.

RELIGIOUS WAR AND THE INTENSIFICATION OF RELIGIOUS HATREDS

By 1562, the theological differences between French Catholics and Protestants had become thoroughly entangled with political rivalries. This does not mean that religious issues had become lesser problems. Because religion was the fundamental mechanism through which people interpreted, or gave meaning, to their world in early modern times, it is impossible to neatly separate religion and politics. Of course, some people chose sides in the war out of calculated self-interest or gain, but the prevailing motivation on both sides was a fundamentally religious one. Protestants and Catholics alike interpreted their political allegiances in terms of obedience to God's will and believed they were fighting to ensure God's will on earth and access to salvation and eternal life for themselves and their fellow citizens. This made the stakes in the war very high.

When the first war broke out in March 1562, Catherine de Medici hesitated between the two sides, uncertain how best to protect twelve-year-old Charles IX's authority. But Condé, in retreating to Orléans, rejected her overtures. Forced into an uneasy alliance with the duke of Guise and other Catholic princes, Catherine nevertheless continued to attempt to negotiate peace. Meanwhile, the Huguenots followed up the seizure of Orléans by capturing other defensible towns at strategic points on road and river systems. They staged revolts in key cities such as Lyons and Rouen and took still others through military action.

Huguenot revolts were most successful in the south, where Calvinism had made the deepest inroads. By May, most of Guyenne, Dauphiné, and Languedoc were in Huguenot hands; only the key cities of Toulouse and Bordeaux eluded the Protestants. Some of the takeovers were accomplished peacefully, but many involved violence on both sides. Where successful, the Huguenots took over churches and city governments, prohibiting Catholic worship and frequently forcing Catholic elites to flee. Protestant crowds engaged in iconoclastic sprees, destroying altars, relics, and other objects the Catholics held as holy. Meanwhile, cities such as Paris that remained in Catholic hands expelled members of the opposing faith and violently attacked anyone suspected of siding with the enemy. Civil war was thus not just being fought on the battlefield, and making peace would require pacifying cities and not just convincing military leaders to lay down their weapons after they reached a stalemate in the field.

Catherine's attempts to negotiate a compromise succeeded in March 1563. The Protestants may have been numerically weak, but they still held enough cities that the Catholics could not afford to fight on. The Peace of Amboise promised Protestants freedom of conscience but permitted them to worship only in certain circumstances. Protestant nobles could hold private religious services on the estates where they resided, but public worship was permitted only in cities that Protestants held at the end of the war and in the suburbs of one town in each governmental district. The edict also attempted to put an end to the desire for revenge that each side harbored against the other by consigning the past to oblivion.

It nevertheless proved easier to legislate oblivion than to enforce it. Both sides were unhappy with the settlement and demonstrated this by their reluctance to comply with the edict's terms. Catholics were angry because the edict allowed the continued existence of two religions in the kingdom, and they often refused to allow Protestants who had fled in the war to return to their homes or resume official functions, as the edict promised they might. Protestants, meanwhile, proved just as unwilling to restore the Mass in cities they controlled as Catholics were to accept even the limited right to public worship accorded Huguenots by the peace. Protestants also remained aggrieved because the Peace of Amboise gave them less opportunity for worship than they had enjoyed under the edict of January 1562.

Chafing under these restrictions and convinced that Catholic leaders were only biding their time and waiting for the proper moment to eliminate Protestant worship altogether, the Huguenots took up arms again in 1567. Francis, duke of Guise, had been assassinated at the end of the first religious war, but his brother Charles, cardinal of Lorraine, had achieved a dominant position at court. Determining once again to "rescue" the king from his anti-Protestant advisers, Huguenot leaders planned to seize Charles IX while he was hunting outside Paris at Meaux. As at Amboise, word of the conspiracy leaked out in advance. The king hastily summoned reinforcements and retreated to the security of his capital (Document 12).

Although Huguenot leaders later claimed that they had sought only to meet with the king and not to kidnap him, the fact that they had simultaneously seized towns elsewhere in France made it impossible for the king and queen mother to doubt their treacherous intentions.

Horribles cruautez des Huguenots en France.

π

La rage des malings ne laiſſe etre en repos
Les os ſacrez des ſainĉts aux ſepulchres enclos,
O rebelles mutins, en meſpriſants les loix!
Leurs corps enſeueliz par pluſieurs ans paſſez
Brulé tu as en cendre, & puis en l'air ieclez,
N'ayant aucun reſpect aux Seigneurs ny aux Roys.

Horrible Cruelties of the Huguenots in France

This image of Protestants burning a Catholic church and breaking up the art and tombs in another church was part of a series of prints, *Horrible Cruelties of the Huguenots in France*, published by Richard Verstegan in his *Theater of the Cruelties of the Heretics of Our Time* (Antwerp, 1587). The verses below the image read: "The rage of the wicked does not leave to rest / The sacred bones of the saints enclosed in their tombs, / O mutinous rebels, despising the laws! / Their bodies entombed for some years past / You have burned into ashes and thrown to the winds / Having no respect for lords or kings."

Bibliothèque nationale de France.

In the long term, the Huguenots' failed attempt to seize Charles IX at Meaux was an important reason why the king and his mother reacted so decisively when the rumor spread that Protestants planned another attempt to seize the king in August 1572. In the shorter term, the "surprise of Meaux" touched off the second civil war.

This time there was no question which side the crown would take. With their attempt to capture the king, the Huguenots were rebels and aggressors. Their blockade of Paris made the capital and its hinterland the focus of the ensuing war, though fighting also took place in provincial towns contested by opposing parties. Parisians lived through the war in a state of heightened dread, convinced that the Huguenots planned to enter the city and burn it to the ground. Despite their fear, the city's residents strongly opposed the queen mother's attempts to negotiate a settlement. They wanted to fight to the end, so as to eliminate the problem of heresy once and for all. But Catherine had good reasons for seeking a compromise; she simply could not afford the cost of keeping an army in the field until a decisive victory was secured.

This was the mechanism that drove the hostilities on, such that there were eight civil wars before the Edict of Nantes brought a more stable peace in 1598. Superior numbers gave the Catholics an advantage in the field, but the Huguenots undermined this advantage by their strategy of taking widely scattered towns. Siege warfare was expensive and favored the defender. Time and again, Catholic leaders were forced to abandon their hope for a decisive victory. The exact terms of each settlement varied, depending on the relative strength of the opposing forces at the time an agreement was reached, but each peace left at least one side aggrieved and ready to return to the fray as soon as it thought it could gain some new advantage.

The settlement that ended the second war in March 1568 reestablished the compromise Peace of Amboise with only a few changes. One new provision, however, further infuriated Catholics. This was the crown's promise that it would pay the cost of foreign mercenaries hired to fight for the Huguenots. This was necessary because unpaid mercenaries tended to live off the land, wreaking havoc on civilian populations. It nevertheless enraged Catholic citizens to pay for armies that had made war against them. Continuing tensions meant that neither side truly disarmed, and a third War of Religion broke out before the year was over.

Meanwhile, positions were hardening on both sides of the religious divide. Not content merely to outlaw expressions of the Protestant faith, Catholic militants wanted the Huguenots to pay with their lives

for the trouble they had caused. For their part, the Protestants justified taking up arms in strident tones and began to articulate a theory
of the right to resist illegitimate authority that came to full fruition
after the Saint Bartholomew's Day Massacre. Personal enmities also
became more bitter. When Condé was taken prisoner during the first
war, Francis, duke of Guise, upholding ancient traditions of noble
honor, had treated Condé courteously and even shared his meals and
lodging with his captive. When Condé was injured in the third war, he
again surrendered to a Catholic nobleman. This time, instead of being
received courteously, he was shot in the head, and his corpse was
flung over a donkey and paraded derisively into the Catholic camp.
Meanwhile, in Paris, the Huguenots' other leader, Admiral Gaspard de
Coligny, was tried in absentia for treason and sedition and, having
been judged guilty, executed in effigy. In the admiral's absence, the
rituals of execution to which he had been sentenced were enacted on
a straw dummy painted with his features for the pleasure of the crowd
(Document 13).

As in previous cases, the Huguenots began the third war at a disad-
vantage in numbers but rallied to negotiate from a position of strength.
The Peace of Saint-Germain (August 1570) granted Protestants an
additional place of worship in every province or government and, recognizing that anger stirred up in the quarrels would be slow to abate,
promised them four fortified cities to be used as places of refuge for
two years, after which they were to be surrendered back to the crown.
Many Catholics considered these provisions entirely too favorable to
the Huguenots. They also resented the explicit demand to forget the
quarrels and obliterate all memory of them.

A monument in Paris known as the Cross of Gastines became a
particular bone of contention (Document 14). A tall pyramid topped by
a cross, it commemorated the destruction of a house belonging to the
merchants Richard and Philippe de Gastines, who were executed in
1569 on the charge of illegally celebrating the Lord's Supper. When
Coligny returned to court after the peace and reversal of the judgment
against him, he insisted that the monument be torn down in compliance
with the Peace of Saint-Germain. The Parisian populace, stirred up by
radical preachers who likened removal of the cross to a betrayal of
Christ, refused to let this happen. Tensions grew through the fall of
1571. Riots broke out in December after the king, in an attempt at
compromise, ordered the cross removed to a nearby cemetery instead
of being entirely destroyed. Although much smaller in scale and less
violent than the Saint Bartholomew's Day Massacre, the riots over the

Cross of Gastines presaged the massacre in important ways. Huguenots whose houses were pillaged in these riots were among the first non-nobles attacked on Saint Bartholomew's Day. On both occasions, moreover, the professional troops available to assist city officials in keeping the peace proved inadequate, and yet arming the Parisian citizenry caused other problems. Many simply could not be trusted to protect the homes and property of people they regarded as heretics and enemies.

The tensions stirred up by the Cross of Gastines affair did not disappear. Paris remained on edge through the spring of 1572, its citizens reacting angrily to every sign of favor that Charles IX appeared to show the Huguenots. People knew that the king was considering aiding a Huguenot army that had invaded the Netherlands in May 1572 in support of Dutch Protestants, who had rebelled against their sovereign, King Philip II of Spain. Although Spain was France's hereditary enemy, Catholic Parisians feared the danger and cost of an international war, and they hated the idea of allying with heretics against a Catholic king. They also hated Charles's plan to marry his sister, Marguerite of Valois, to the Protestant prince Henry of Bourbon, king of Navarre. Dynastic alliances were a traditional practice among European monarchs, and Charles's expressed hope was to further cement the Peace of Saint-Germain by tightening the bonds between the royal family and the Huguenot leadership.[6] For Parisian Catholics, however, the religiously mixed marriage was an impious alliance for which God would surely be avenged. Many took the events that occurred in the wake of the wedding, which was celebrated on August 18, 1572, as confirmation of this prophecy, for the marriage brought large numbers of Huguenot gentlemen to Paris, thereby setting the stage for their subsequent massacre.

THE SAINT BARTHOLOMEW'S DAY MASSACRE IN PARIS AND THE PROVINCES

The wedding involved elaborate festivities—tournaments, costume balls, and other entertainments—but also gave Admiral Coligny the opportunity once again to lobby the king to aid the Protestants fighting in the Netherlands. The trouble began when a would-be assassin fired on Coligny as he returned from a meeting with Charles IX on the morning of August 22. A chance move on the admiral's part saved his life by confining the injuries to a hand and arm. Huguenot leaders nevertheless reacted angrily, blaming the Guises and insisting on retribution (Document 15). The accusation was grounded in old rivalries but also in the known fact that the house from which the shot had come belonged to a Guise family retainer. The Huguenots' initial claim has been much disputed. Some observers instead blame the king's own mother, Catherine de Medici, on the grounds that she was jealous of Coligny's increasing influence with Charles IX and fearful that he would drag France into a dangerous war with Spain. According to the Venetian ambassador, "The whole thing was the work of the queen" (Document 16). The accusation is puzzling but hard to dismiss. As a woman and a foreigner, Catherine was vulnerable. Her enemies denounced her as a Machiavellian Italian capable of any deceit, and yet everything she had worked for in the previous months and years aimed at the pacification of religious tensions and not their inflammation, as a strike against Coligny was bound to cause. Would she really have changed tactics so suddenly and dramatically?

We will never know for certain who was behind the attack on Coligny. In the end, however, the question of who was responsible for this initial shot pales before the chain of events it touched off. As word of the attack spread around the city, the Huguenots' angry response was thought to portend a Protestant uprising. A rumor that Protestant troops waited outside the city for the signal to seize the royal family and avenge themselves against their enemies drove tensions to a fever pitch. Although there was no truth to the story, it appears to have been widely believed, even in the highest circles (Document 17). Or perhaps, as some have claimed, the purported threat of a Huguenot coup was merely an excuse to purge France of a troublesome minority. Whatever the crown's intentions, late in the evening of August 23 a preemptive strike was ordered against not only Coligny but also the rest of the Huguenot leadership. Early the next morning, Saint Bartholomew's Day by the church calendar, Henry, duke of Guise, led troops to Coligny's lodgings to finish the murder attempted two days earlier. After killing the admiral, the duke's men tossed his body out the window, so that Guise, waiting below, might confirm his identity. The corpse was later mutilated and dragged through the streets by riotous youths.

Meanwhile, members of the king's guard and other bands of soldiers set out to find and kill other Huguenot leaders quartered in the city. The noise they made in a night already tense with fear touched off a wave of popular violence. The duke of Guise, urging his men on, was heard to say that they killed by the king's express command.

These words quickly spread through the populace, who took them as permission—even an order—to rid themselves of the pollution of heresy by slaughtering their Protestant neighbors. Members of the civic militia, stationed about the streets to help keep order, were among the first to take up their weapons against the Protestants, but other citizens joined in as well.

Although some observers accused city officials of abetting the killing, other sources suggest that they tried to keep order but were overwhelmed by the popular violence. City records confirm that they stationed militia companies around the city on the night of August 23, but these records suggest that the militia's intended mission was to ward off an anticipated Huguenot coup and not to attack Protestant civilians (Document 18). The following morning, city officials protested to the king that "a number of persons attached both to His Majesty and to the princes, princesses, and grandees of the court, . . . along with all sorts of other people who had joined with them and used their cover, were pillaging and sacking houses and killing people in the streets."[7] The king in reply instructed officials to mount a patrol with city troops so as to put an end to the unrest. They organized the patrol and issued orders forbidding anyone to harm the Protestants or pillage their property. The following day, they sent out district officers to make a list of everyone residing in their district and instruct householders to protect Protestant lodgers. None of these efforts stanched the wave of violence, which continued for most of a week, and some had negative consequences. The list of names, for example, appears to have been used to round up and imprison Protestants—in theory to protect them, but more often resulting in their deaths. Whether city officials acted in good faith and whether they could have done more must remain open questions, and we should be wary of easy generalizations. Surely, some officials did work hard to calm the situation and protect vulnerable Protestants (Document 20), but others were negligent and tolerated or even supported the violence.

Many of the killings had a didactic or ritual character. Killers forced their victims to recant their faith or repeat Catholic prayers and made bonfires of Protestant books. They also subjected their victims' bodies to crude parodies of religious and judicial rites. We read of infants "baptized" in the blood of their parents or cut from their mothers' wombs and "baptized" in the Seine. The youths who dragged Coligny's corpse through city streets are reported to have conducted his trial as they dragged him along. Repeating their sentence against him at major crossroads, they burned his body in a parody of the conventional punishment for heretics and tossed it into the river, from which it was eventually retrieved and hung from the gallows where common criminals were put to death. If some of the killers attempted to convert their victims or reenacted rites of purification, others seized the opportunity to settle private scores or even to profit from their victims' distress. Looting and pillaging were common; so was extortion. Women, especially if pregnant, appear to have suffered particularly gruesome deaths (Document 20). Was this because their murderers saw their bodies as vessels for the propagation of heresy? Or did Protestant chroniclers linger over these stories because they so clearly evoked the profound sense of victimization the massacre entailed?

We should not assume that all Parisian Catholics participated in the violence. Probably most remained behind locked doors, not daring to venture out until the killings were over. Bolder ones hid Huguenot neighbors and helped them to escape. Many of those who escaped were aided at one or more points by Catholics who hid them and concealed their flight (Document 21). Henry, duke of Guise, was the most famous but not the only Catholic aristocrat to shelter Protestant fugitives. This appears paradoxical, given Guise's notorious role in the assassination of the Huguenot leadership, but it is not in fact contradictory if the initial intention was to eliminate the Protestants' military leaders and not to slaughter the Huguenot population at large.

The king's role in the massacre remains a mystery. Most historians believe that he ordered the killings only under duress, convinced by his mother and other members of his council of the need to make a surgical strike against the Huguenots before they could mount their own coup against the crown. There is little agreement, however, about his subsequent behavior or intentions. Some Protestant propagandists depicted him as an enthusiastic participant in the killing (Document 22); other accounts say that he kept to himself and took no part. The explanations he gave provincial governors, foreign heads of state, and magistrates of his Parlement contradict one another. He first tried to blame the Guises or pass the whole thing off as an accident, the result of popular furies that got out of hand. When he realized that many Catholics at home and abroad were celebrating the massacre rather than condemning it, he stepped forward to take credit for it, telling the Parlement that "all that occurred was by his express commandment" (Document 23). He even had a medal struck depicting him as Hercules slaying the Hydra of heresy.

The king's contradictory messages helped perpetuate the massacre in Paris and spread the violence to other cities. Although Charles sent letters to provincial governors urging them to take strict measures to keep the peace, officials in some towns claimed to have received just the opposite message by word of mouth. There is no evidence that Charles actually sent such orders, but elsewhere, as in Paris, there were people willing to act on the belief that the king wished the Protestants killed. By early October, the murders had spread to at least a dozen major provincial cities, including Lyons, Rouen, Bordeaux, and Toulouse, and had cost another two thousand to three thousand people their lives, in addition to Paris's estimated two thousand to three thousand victims.

The killings were worst in the cities that had suffered most from the religious conflicts of the previous decade. A thousand people died in Orléans, for example. A university town of 45,000 to 50,000 people, Orléans was the first city the Huguenots had seized in 1562 and one they had subsequently lost. Although excluded from power, the Protestants clearly represented a more threatening minority and were the object of more virulent hatred here than in provincial cities where peace was maintained. As in Paris, hesitation on the part of top officials allowed the initiative in Orléans to fall into the hands of the more radical members of the citizenry, particularly among the civic guard, and a variety of personal motives—including both old enmities and greed—fueled the religious violence (Document 24). The same was true in Troyes, where people began to attack Protestants in the streets as soon as they heard word of the massacre in Paris, without waiting for orders from the king.

Protestant accounts from Orléans and Troyes insist that local officials there did receive orders to exterminate the Huguenot population, even if these orders arrived only after the killing had begun, but how far can these accounts be trusted? These Protestant authors were in no position to see the documents in question and had to rely on rumors that, one suspects, they were only too willing to credit. If the account from Troyes can be believed, the order to kill that city's Huguenots came from the provincial governor, the duke of Guise, and was transmitted orally by the messenger the city had sent to confirm reports from Paris. When the news was conveyed to the mayor and city council, "a number of members of the council were astonished at this cruel order," and "those who did not want to consent to it withdrew" (Document 25). This withdrawal on the part of moderates in Troyes, which left the initiative in the hands of more zealous citizens, contrasts strikingly with what occurred in Limoges, where city officials drew together while awaiting orders from Paris and resolved to take every precaution to keep the peace. They did this because they were

Medal Struck to Celebrate Charles IX's Victory over the Huguenots
The medal credits Charles with conquering the rebels on one side and depicts
him as Hercules slaying the Hydra of heresy on the other.
Bibliothèque nationale de France.

unsure what the king wanted, but also because they were afraid that if
people took up arms, they might use them "not only against those of
the [new] religion, but rather against the principal residents who were
rumored to have well-stocked houses or stores" (Document 26).
Although self-preservation, rather than religious tolerance, seems to
have motivated Limoges's citizens to spare the city's small Huguenot
population, the episode does reveal that city officials resolutely determined to prevent violence might have succeeded in doing so.

REPERCUSSIONS OF THE MASSACRE
IN FRANCE AND ABROAD

Even beyond the four thousand to six thousand persons who died as a
direct result of the events known collectively as the Saint Bartholomew's
Day Massacre, these events had a devastating effect on the Reformed
church in France. Church membership declined precipitously; one
minister later claimed that Reformed churches lost two-thirds of their
members in the wake of this disaster. Many survivors emigrated,
believing it simply too dangerous to remain in France. Geneva in particular received a new wave of immigrants. An even larger number of

French Protestants returned to the Catholic Church. A chronicler from Troyes, for example, lamented that "there remained in the city only twenty [people] who retained their purity and did not pollute themselves with the abominations of the papacy" (Document 27). Some were converted by force, but others simply lost confidence in their beliefs and their identity as God's chosen children. They could accept the idea that God would test their faith, but not that he could allow their slaughter (Document 28).

Many ardent Catholics also interpreted the massacre as a punishment from God, but unlike the Huguenots, they celebrated the success of the coup as a sign of God's hatred for heresy and a promise that the unity of the church would be restored (Document 29). When a hawthorn tree in a Parisian cemetery suddenly bloomed out of season, Parisians rushed to view the "miracle" and interpreted it as a sign of divine favor. Protestant commentators suspected trickery but were in no position to prove their claims.

The rejoicing of French Catholics was echoed in foreign capitals when word of the massacre spread abroad (Document 30). Masses were sung at the Spanish court and in Rome, where Gregory XIII, recently elected pope, commissioned two more permanent commemorations of Saint Bartholomew's Day. The first was a medal celebrating the extirpation of the Huguenots, with a bust of the pope on one side and an avenging angel on the other. Similar in content if not in scale were three frescoes that Gregory commissioned from Giorgio Vasari for the Sala Regia in the Vatican palace, the room where the pope formally received ambassadors and kings.

Not all Catholic leaders reacted with the same enthusiasm. The Holy Roman emperor Maximilian II's principal reaction was a dismay made all the more acute by the fact that he had married his daughter to Charles IX. The massacre would never have happened, he wrote Elector August of Saxony, if his son-in-law had consulted him first: "To settle religious disputes by the sword or through force is neither possible nor morally justifiable."[8] Though couched in terms of moral absolutes, Maximilian's position was in effect a defensive one. His empire was divided, and he feared that the massacre might destabilize its tenuous religious peace. It is, moreover, striking that neither he nor other German princes publicly chastised Charles IX or broke off diplomatic relations with France. Nor did England's Protestant Queen Elizabeth, although her courtiers did make a silent protest by dressing in mourning and stonily refusing to acknowledge the presence of France's ambassador when he first reappeared at court.

Medal Struck in Rome to Commemorate the Massacre
Pope Gregory XIII had this medal struck with his own portrait on one side and an avenging angel, sword in hand, advancing on a crowd of dead, dying, and fleeing Huguenots on the other. The inscription, *"Ugonottorum Strages 24 Augusti Anno 1572,"* lauds the extirpation of the Huguenots. Although several women are included among the fallen, the depiction of a broken sword in the hand of one Huguenot and fallen weapons at the feet of others suggest that the Huguenots were killed in battle and not murdered in their beds.
Bibliothèque nationale de France.

Within a short time, publicists began to tell the story of Saint Bartholomew's Day from a variety of points of view. Just two months after the massacre, a papal courtier named Camillo Capilupi rushed a narrative titled *The Stratagem of Charles IX* into print in Italian. Crediting the king with cleverly leading the Huguenots into a trap, the work reflects the joy with which many committed Catholics greeted the first news of the massacre. No documents have ever surfaced to substantiate Capilupi's claim of premeditation, and the work is now viewed as part of the propaganda campaign issuing from the massacre rather than as a factual account of events. Its claims of premeditation nevertheless reinforced the already strong conviction in Protestant circles that the murders had been plotted in advance. Protestant writers quickly translated the pamphlet into French and, reversing its original intent, used it to denounce the king's treachery.

A number of Protestant-authored accounts of the massacre also appeared, for it was the Huguenots who had the strongest incentive to recount the outrages they had suffered. Despite the decimation of their leadership, French Protestants believed they had no choice but to respond to the massacre by a return to arms. Retreating to La Rochelle, the most easily defended of the strongholds awarded them by the Peace of Saint-Germain, they prepared to fight a fourth religious war. The war was brief; the Huguenots lacked the money and men to pose a serious challenge to the royal armies that besieged them. Unable to hold out for long, they accepted a punitive settlement that cut back their right to worship, but they secretly began to plan to fight again under more favorable circumstances.

At the same time, they began to publicize the horrors of Saint Bartholomew's Day not only to gain foreign sympathy—and potentially financial support—for their cause but also to justify their rebellion, reassure the faithful, and attempt to draw apostates back to the Reformed church. Most of the publicity was done through words and not images, but one anonymous German print, though based on printed sources and not firsthand experience of the massacre, memorably captures the horror of the event (Document 31). Of broader political resonance were the theories justifying resistance to tyranny elaborated in the wake of the massacre.

Prior to Saint Bartholomew's Day, the Huguenots had tried to deny—or at least to play down—accusations of rebellion against the crown. They had portrayed the plot to seize Francis II at Amboise as an attempt to save the king from the "tyrant Guises," for example, and not an act of sedition. Even after trying to seize Charles IX at Meaux, thereby touching off the second religious war, the Huguenots insisted that they opposed the king's evil advisers and not the king himself. Once Charles IX claimed credit for ordering the Saint Bartholomew's Day Massacre, such proclamations of loyalty were no longer tenable. Forced to articulate a new rationale for going to war, Huguenot spokesmen argued that resistance to royal authority was justified when the king behaved like a tyrant. The events of Saint Bartholomew's Day became prime evidence and justification for revolt. The right of resistance was elaborated in cautiously stated treatises by humanist scholars such as François Hotman (also the author of the often reprinted *True and Plain Report of the Furious Outrages of France*; Document 15) and Theodore de Bèze with little or no direct reference to contemporary events. But it was also advanced in a more direct fashion in polemics such as *The Wake-Up Call for the French and Their Neighbors*, which sought to gain support for the Huguenots' revolt both within France and internationally by justifying their taking up arms within the explicit context of the Saint Bartholomew's Day Massacre (Document 32).

In contrast to theorists of absolutism, who taught that kings were chosen by God, Huguenot resistance theorists located the origins of political authority in a compact between people and their kings. This gave the people the right to refuse to obey a king if the king broke the compact by abusing his authority. Resistance theory soon lost out in France to the competing theory of royal absolutism. The near anarchy experienced during the Wars of Religion made people place a high value on stability. They accepted the idea that kings were absolute as a way of strengthening royal authority, rather than risk limiting this authority by positing a right to resist a king's commands. The arguments that Huguenot theorists made about the constitutional origins of political authority nevertheless had a lasting impact. They reemerged in the social contract theory of John Locke and other constitutionalists in seventeenth-century England.

The Huguenots were not the only ones to reassess their political position in the wake of Saint Bartholomew's Day. The violence of the massacre polarized French Catholics and caused a realignment of political factions. While Catholic militants applauded the coup as a necessary step toward eliminating heresy entirely from the kingdom, Catholic moderates, horrified by the slaughter, argued for peace even at the price of toleration and a perpetuation of the religious divisions.[9] In 1574, a group of moderates, known as Malcontents because of their dissatisfaction with royal policies, even allied with the Huguenots to make war against the crown. Bowing to the coalition's force, Henry III (formerly the duke of Anjou), who succeeded his brother Charles IX on the latter's death in 1574, agreed to peace in 1576 on generous terms that pleased the Huguenots with increased security and rights to worship. He also cleverly separated their erstwhile allies from them through political patronage and promises of reform. In contrast, the generous rights extended to the Huguenots prompted a new anger among zealous Catholics. Banding together as the Holy League, dedicated to the elimination of heresy, Catholic militants forced Henry III into yet another religious war, followed by yet another troubled peace. Exhaustion and lack of funds allowed the cessation of hostilities to continue until 1585, when the religious wars entered their last painful stage with the wars of the Holy League.

As France's religious divisions deepened, they also took on broader European dimensions. In the Netherlands, Dutch Calvinists fighting to shake off the yoke of Catholic Spain forged a militantly Protestant identity for themselves as they battled to create an independent state in the northern provinces. After some hesitation, the southern provinces promised loyalty to Spain and became ardently Catholic; Protestant converts fled to the north. Confessional hatreds were inflamed as the war for Dutch independence took on the character of a religious war, and both Protestants and Catholics recounted horrors from France's religious conflicts as evidence of their enemies' inhumanity. Richard Verstegan's *Theater of the Cruelties of the Heretics of Our Time*, first published in Catholic Antwerp in 1587, graphically illustrated various atrocities—disembowelment, burning alive, and other tortures—allegedly perpetrated by Protestants against their Catholic enemies in France, the Netherlands, and the British Isles (Document 33). Verstegan had previously been involved in the underground publication of Catholic martyrologies in England but had fled the country in fear of arrest. England was establishing its own Protestant identity, and persecution of Catholics at home and hatred of them abroad were becoming important elements in this identity.

International alliances reflected these deepening religious divisions. England's Queen Elizabeth first clandestinely and then more openly aided Protestant rebels in both France and the Netherlands. Her efforts eventually prompted King Philip II of Spain to send an armada of more than a hundred ships with the intention of invading England, deposing Elizabeth, and restoring the Catholic Church. Launched in 1588, Philip's great armada was defeated at sea. Elizabeth's throne was saved, but the conflicts reinforced anti-Spanish and anti-Catholic sentiment in the island nation. They also complicated France's religious quarrels by raising the specter of an international religious war.

The situation in France had reached a crisis point in 1584, when Henry III's younger brother and presumed heir, Francis, duke of Anjou (formerly duke of Alençon)[10] died, leaving the Protestant prince Henry of Bourbon, king of Navarre, as heir presumptive to the French throne.[11] Refusing to accept the possibility of a Protestant king, zealous Catholics insisted that Henry III declare Navarre ineligible to succeed to the crown. The king refused, rightly claiming that he had no authority to alter the line of succession. Angered by his refusal, the radicals revived the Holy League and forced Henry III to formally declare his intention of putting an end to heresy. In July 1585, he signed a treaty revoking previous edicts of toleration and forbidding exercise of the Reformed faith. The war that subsequently broke out was an odd, three-cornered struggle that began with Henry III allied with the armies of the Holy League against the Huguenots. Henry III chafed, however, at the growing power of Henry, duke of Guise, who headed the league. Chased from his capital in May 1588 by popular demonstrations in favor of the duke of Guise, Henry III took his revenge six months later by ordering the duke assassinated by his guard at Blois. Intended to preserve Henry's III's crown, the gesture put it even more at risk, as leading aristocrats, provinces, and cities went into open rebellion against him. Reconciling with Navarre so as to gain his support in making war against the Holy League, Henry III officially recognized the Protestant prince as his successor shortly before dying by an assassin's knife in August 1589. The murderer struck because he thought Henry too soft on the Huguenots, and yet his mortal blow brought a Protestant to the throne.

Claiming the crown as Henry IV, Navarre had to fight to make good his claim. The opposition had grown stronger on Henry III's death, as some moderate Catholics had defected to the league rather than accept a Protestant king. Meanwhile, radical Catholics entered into an alliance with Spain and invited Philip II to send troops to aid the fight against Henry IV. To weaken the opposition and become more acceptable to his subjects, the vast majority of whom were Catholics, Henry IV announced in 1593 that he would take instruction in the Catholic faith. His motives for converting are cynically summed up in the aphorism "Paris is worth a Mass." Contrary to popular legend, Henry never said such a thing. His enemies merely claimed that he had so as to undermine the legitimacy of his conversion. Despite continued opposition, Henry proved victorious on the battlefield. One by one, cities and provinces surrendered to him. The biggest rush came after Paris surrendered in March 1594, but a few stragglers held out for another four years.

Henry was generous in peace, rewarding his former enemies with large pensions as well as promises of amnesty. Only a handful of the most virulent Holy League leaders and publicists suffered exile or other punishments for their rebellion. This offended Huguenot leaders, who worried about what Henry's conversion might mean for their own place in the kingdom. Solemnly consecrated and crowned in February 1594 after his formal abjuration, Henry IV, like his predecessors, took an oath requiring him to expel all heretics so designated by the church. How would he square this oath with his obligation to the former coreligionists who had fought alongside him for so many years? Still militarily powerful, Huguenot leaders worked hard to negotiate a settlement that would guarantee both security and the right to worship. Their efforts resulted in the Edict of Nantes, which they accepted in April 1598 (Document 34), although it took Henry IV another year to convince the Parlement to officially accept and register the law (Document 35).

Like the religious settlements that preceded it, the Edict of Nantes failed to fully satisfy either side. It promised the Huguenots freedom of conscience but allowed public worship only in specified places. It also set out elaborate provisions for adjudicating disputes between members of contrary faiths. In addition, the king allowed the Huguenots to garrison nearly two hundred fortified towns, half of them at the crown's expense, for a period of eight years. If most of the clauses in the Edict of Nantes reiterated provisions in earlier settlements, there was one significant difference this time around. Unlike his weaker predecessors, Henry IV intended the peace to be observed.

The Edict of Nantes is justly celebrated as a momentous achievement. If it did not provide a permanent end to the religious quarrels—the Huguenots went to war again in the 1620s and lost the right to hold fortified towns—it nevertheless provided a productive interval of peace. Under the terms of the edict, religious coexistence operated relatively well within many local communities. For the most part, Protestants and Catholics led separate lives, mingling largely in public spaces, but over time a certain amount of social integration took place. The edict could not, however, put a final end to religious dissension, for the underlying causes of that dissension had not disappeared. Neither Protestants nor Catholics had abandoned the idea that they—and only they—represented the true church. They had agreed to stop fighting but did not cease trying to convert members of the other religion through preaching, propaganda, and theological debate. Religious controversy did not disappear. Quite the contrary, the spread of the Catholic Reformation to France in the early seventeenth century prompted the foundation of militant new religious orders and fervent missions to evangelize the French countryside. The missions appear to have gained relatively few outright converts, but they did succeed in stirring up Catholic fervor—and thus accentuating religious divisions rather than furthering peaceful coexistence.

In the end, however, it was not popular religious discontent but rather royal policy that destroyed the religious toleration mandated by the Edict of Nantes. Raised as a devout Catholic, Henry IV's son, King Louis XIII, went to war against the Huguenots to forcibly restore the Catholic Church where it had been suppressed and to wipe out the Huguenots' military power by depriving them of their fortified towns. This left the Huguenots vulnerable to the aggressive conversion tactics subsequently authorized by Louis XIII's son, Louis XIV, whose determination to centralize authority in the state extended to religious unity as well. When Louis XIV revoked the Edict of Nantes and forbade Protestant worship in 1685, an estimated 150,000 Protestants fled abroad, even though forbidden to leave. Countless others resorted to clandestine worship and secret resistance, just as their ancestors had a century earlier. Regaining their civil rights only on the eve of the French Revolution, French Protestants continued to nurture a distinctive identity, rooted in their faith but also in historical memories that set them apart from the mass of their co-citizens and that tended to leave them critical of absolute authority and favorable toward minority rights.

MEMORIES OF THE MASSACRE

Historical memory recalls the massacre in three distinct but related ways: as a story of the persecution of French Protestants, as a tale of royal treachery, and as a warning against intolerance. From the beginning, French Protestants had identified with David against the Catholic Goliath and viewed persecution as a trial imposed by God and a mark of his covenant. After the shock of Saint Bartholomew's Day, they built upon and expanded the image of themselves as a chosen people by collecting accounts of their suffering in histories and martyrologies (Document 20). Despite the sad truth that many Huguenots did recant under the pressure of the massacre, they presented themselves as a people whose faith could be tested but not broken.

Seventeenth-century Catholic writers looked back on the massacre through different eyes. Most histories of France by Catholic authors took up the crown's argument that the massacre was a necessary response to a planned Huguenot coup. At the same time, the image of Charles IX as a tyrant-king, first evoked by Huguenot publicists, survived and even grew in importance as the negative image with which Henry IV and subsequent Bourbon kings might be compared. Louis XIV's historians, for example, used Charles IX as an object lesson in bad kingship. Depicting him as poorly educated and badly raised, corrupted by his foreign mother and her decadent court, they made of him the very antithesis of the Bourbon kings, who knew how to be obeyed and brought peace and order to their troubled realm. To drive the lesson home, they borrowed from the Protestant *Wake-Up Call* the dubious story of Charles IX personally firing on fleeing Huguenots (Document 22).

The same image was used to discredit monarchy entirely at the time of the French Revolution. During the Revolution's most radical stage, for example, journalist Jean-Paul Marat justified the popular violence then occurring in Paris with an explicit comparison to Saint Bartholomew's Day: "What are the few drops of blood that the populace has spilled in the current revolution by comparison with the torrents . . . that the mystical frenzy of a Charles IX caused to be spread."[12] The image also featured prominently in nineteenth-century histories and novels, precisely because the whole problem of monarchy remained a subject of debate. Alexandre Dumas's 1845 novel *Marguerite de Valois*, for instance, features a dramatic scene in which Charles IX, "ghastly as a corpse, his eyes injected with blood," fires furiously at the Huguenots, "uttering cries of joy every time his aim was successful."[13] Such narratives of royal treachery tended to portray Charles IX as weak and unbalanced. They completed the gender reversal by depicting Catherine de Medici as the scheming power behind the throne—a woman usurping a man's role. At the same time, they played on her "womanly weakness" by attributing her actions to an obsessive and even unnatural maternal love.

These exaggerated portraits of Catherine and Charles can still sometimes be found in popular literature and films. Of greater long-term historical significance is the gradual emergence of the massacre as a prime example of and warning against the dangers of intolerance. From the beginning, the massacre was a shocking event. If some Catholics celebrated it as a necessary strike against heresy, others deplored it and wanted the religious conflicts to end, even if it meant tolerating the existence of the Reformed church in France. At this point, however, "toleration" was understood only in the most limited sense of putting up with something one did not like but could not change. It did not mean accepting that the deeply held beliefs of others could be as valid and deserving of recognition as one's own. This broader notion of religious tolerance could only emerge after people were willing to abandon their claims to the unique possession of religious truth.

The philosopher Michel de Montaigne took an important step in this direction as he explored the question "What do I know?" at length in his *Essays*. Montaigne experienced the Wars of Religion firsthand; they ravaged his native Bordelais, leaving him disillusioned and skeptical about claims to superior truth (Document 36). Both parties, he observed, "were so identical in excesses and injustices" that they made it hard to believe that they really were quarreling over essential matters of religious truth. Religious belief remained important to Montaigne as he contemplated the limits of human reason. He remained a committed Christian and a Catholic, and yet the very logic with which he justified remaining in the religion of his ancestors implicitly admitted that he did this for human reasons—because he was "born in a country where it was in practice"—and not because he had any certain knowledge of its superior truth. Montaigne's admission that being born in another region or having different experiences "might imprint upon us in the same way a contrary belief" was a big step toward the modern idea of religious tolerance, because it recognized religious truth as relative and tacitly cautioned against negative judgment or coercion.

Montaigne's skepticism had some faint echoes in the seventeenth century, but only with the eighteenth-century Enlightenment did the moral absolutism of traditional ways of thinking receive a serious challenge. Enlightenment writers criticized the sort of unquestioning belief that previous generations had praised and urged people to think for themselves—to be more open-minded and rational. Religious intolerance became one of their principal targets and religious wars their prime example of the harm intolerance could do. The philosophe Montesquieu, for example, observed "that the history books are full of religious wars; but it should be carefully noted that these wars are not produced by the fact that there is more than one religion, but by the spirit of intolerance, urging on the one which believed itself to be dominant."[14] Voltaire went further. He came to detest all organized religions, believing them responsible for many of society's ills. In the article "War," which Voltaire published in his *Philosophical Dictionary* in 1764, he wrote, "Artificial religion encourages all the cruelties which are committed in company—conspiracies, seditions, pillagings, ambushes, taking towns by surprise, plundering, murders. Everyone marches gaily off to crime under the banner of his saint."[15] The article "Fanaticism," in the same work, explicitly cites the events of Saint Bartholomew's Day as evidence of religion's crimes (Document 37).

In more recent times, the symbolic importance of the Saint Bartholomew's Day Massacre as an evocation of the horrors of intolerance has broadened. This was made clear in 1997, when French Protestants learned that Pope John Paul II would close World Youth Day, being held that year in Paris, with a huge outdoor Mass on Sunday, August 24, a date that coincided with the 425th anniversary of the Saint Bartholomew's Day Massacre. Determined that the tragic events that had occurred on that date should not be overlooked, Protestant youth groups called on the pope to explicitly invoke the memory of the massacre. At the same time, they seized the opportunity to sound a broader call for interfaith dialogue in asking that the memory of the massacre be joined with the evocation of the "current dramas" in Ireland, Algeria, and other countries that were "largely due to religious or ethnic intolerance." They also drew up the Charter for Living Together calling for mutual understanding and respect, which they had signed by members of different faiths (Document 38). The call to remember was heard. The archbishop of Paris and president of the French Bishops' Conference scheduled a "vigil of reconciliation" to which French Protestants were invited on the eve of the international gathering. John Paul II also spoke of his hope for forgiveness and dialogue in his greeting to the crowd of young people gathered for an open-air vigil on the night of August 23 (Document 39). That the pope would use this anniversary of the Saint Bartholomew's Day Massacre to speak of the need for religious tolerance demonstrates well the continuing resonance of this momentous event in our historical consciousness.

NOTES

[1] Until the sixteenth century, Christians living in western Europe saw themselves as belonging to one common church headed by the pope in Rome. The terms *Roman Catholic* and, by extension, just *Catholic* became meaningful only after the Protestant Reformation caused some Christians to renounce their allegiance to Rome and will thus be reserved for that Rome-centered church and the Christians who remained faithful to it once the Protestant schism had begun.

[2] William Monter, *Judging the French Reformation: Heresy Trials by Sixteenth-Century Parlements* (Cambridge, Mass.: Harvard University Press, 1999), 54.

[3] The origins of the word *Huguenot* (pronounced "hyu-ge-nawt" or "hyu-ge-no") are debated. Some consider it a corruption of a term used to describe Swiss mercenaries and hence a reference to the direction from which the new ideas were presumed to come. Others trace it to the ghost named Hugues said to haunt the Loire region and, by extension, to the "ghostly" troops of Protestants gathering to seize the king at Amboise. Whatever its origins, the term was first used as an insult and only later adopted by those against whom it was directed.

[4] A suburb lying outside the city walls.

[5] The Sorbonne was the heart of the prestigious theology faculty of the University of Paris.

[6] Henry had sufficient status to marry into the royal family not because he was king of Navarre, a tiny principality in the Pyrenees, but rather because his paternal lineage as a Bourbon made him first prince of the blood—the highest-ranking French aristocrat after the immediate family of the king.

[7] François Bonnardot, ed., *Registre des délibérations du Bureau de la Ville de Paris* (Paris, 1893), 7:10–15.

[8]Howard Louthan, *The Quest for Compromise: Peacemakers in Counter-Reformation Vienna* (Cambridge: Cambridge University Press, 1997), 51, citing Maximilian's letter of December 13, 1572, as quoted by Viktor Bibl, *Maximilian II: Der Rätselhafte Kaiser; ein Zeitbild* (Hellerau bei Dresden: Avalun, [1929]), 298–99. See also Paula Sutter Fichtner, *Emperor Maximilian II* (New Haven, Conn.: Yale University Press, 2001), 183–86.

[9]These moderates are often called *politiques* because they advocated a political solution to the religious crisis. This was not a term they adopted themselves, but rather one applied by enemies who wanted to discredit the very notion that a political solution to the problem of heresy could exist. It nevertheless has been adopted by historians because it seems to sum up the moderates' position well.

[10]King Henry III had passed his title of duke of Anjou—and the rights and revenues that came with it—to his brother the duke of Alençon in 1576.

[11]By law, the French throne passed exclusively through the male line from eldest son to eldest son. Henry of Navarre's claim to the throne was based on these rules and not his marriage to the king's sister, Marguerite of Valois. Unless Henry III produced a son, which appeared unlikely by 1584, the Valois line would be extinguished on his death. The Bourbons were next in line for the throne, and Henry of Navarre was the eldest son in the eldest branch of this lineage.

[12]*Marat: textes choisis*, ed. Michel Vovelle (Paris: Éditions sociales, 1975), 179.

[13]Alexandre Dumas, *Marguerite de Valois: A Historical Romance* (New York, n.d.), 107–10.

[14]Charles-Louis de Secondat, baron de Montesquieu, *The Persian Letters*, trans. Christopher Betts (Harmondsworth, Eng.: Penguin Books, 1973), 165, letter 85.

[15]Voltaire, *Philosophical Dictionary*, trans. Peter Gay (New York: Basic Books, 1962), 304.

List of Major Figures

Catherine de Medici (1519–1589) Queen of France 1547–1559 and queen mother 1559–1589. The wife of Henry II, she was briefly regent for her son Charles IX and then the power behind the throne through most of his reign and that of Henry III. She has often been accused of taking a leading role in plotting the Saint Bartholomew's Day Massacre.

Charles IX (1550–1574) King of France 1560–1574. He inherited the throne as a child of ten and was just beginning to free himself from his mother's domineering guidance when the massacre broke out. His role in these events is much debated.

Charles of Guise, cardinal of Lorraine (1524–1574) The brother of Francis, duke of Guise, he served the Catholic cause at court and was a leading adviser of Francis II. He was in Rome at the time of the Saint Bartholomew's Day Massacre, but those who believe that the massacre was premeditated tend to assume that he played a role in planning it.

Coligny, Admiral Gaspard de Châtillon (1519–1572) A nephew of Constable Anne de Montmorency, he was the leader of the Huguenots after the death of Louis of Bourbon, prince of Condé, in 1569. An attempt to assassinate him in 1572 touched off the Saint Bartholomew's Day Massacre.

Francis II (1544–1560) King of France 1559–1560. Came to the throne following the accidental death of his father, Henry II, in 1559. During his brief rule, Francis, duke of Guise, and Charles, cardinal of Lorraine, the uncles of Francis II's wife, Mary, Queen of Scots, had great influence at court.

Francis, duke of Alençon (later duke of Anjou) (1555–1584) The youngest son of Henry II and Catherine de Medici; a moderate Catholic whose death in 1584 touched off a succession crisis because it left the Protestant Henry of Navarre next in line for the French throne.

Francis of Lorraine, duke of Guise (1519–1563) A military leader and head of the Catholic faction at court until an assassin took his life during the first War of Religion.

Henry II (1519–1559) King of France 1547–1559. Much of his reign was spent finishing up the wars with Habsburg Germany and Spain begun by his father, Francis I. Making peace with Spain in 1559, he hoped to put an end to the Protestant "heresy" in France but instead died as a result of a jousting accident at the tournament intended to celebrate the peace. His wife, Catherine de Medici, was left to deal with the building factional and religious conflicts on behalf of his young sons.

Henry, duke of Anjou; Henry III of France (1551–1589)   King of France 1574–1589. The third son of Henry II and Catherine de Medici, he won a (probably undeserved) reputation as a military leader in the third War of Religion and was believed by many to have played a more active role on Saint Bartholomew's Day than his brother Charles IX. He proved more moderate and less ardently Catholic once king and came to be opposed by the Holy League, which chased him from Paris in 1588. An ultra-Catholic assassin killed him in 1589.

Henry, duke of Guise (1550–1588)   The son of Francis, duke of Guise, he had begun to assume his father's role as leader of the Catholic faction at the time of the Saint Bartholomew's Day Massacre. Many believed he was behind the initial attempt on Coligny's life because he blamed the admiral for his father's death. The Holy League organized under his leadership subsequently challenged the rule of Henry III, who had him assassinated in 1588.

Henry of Bourbon, king of Navarre; Henry IV of France (1553–1610)   King of Navarre 1572–1610; king of France 1589–1610. His wedding to King Charles IX's sister, Marguerite of Valois, provided the occasion for the Saint Bartholomew's Day Massacre. Raised a Protestant, he was forced to convert after the massacre but returned to the Protestant faith and took on leadership of the Huguenot rebellion once he escaped from court in 1576. As first prince of the blood, he inherited the crown of France when the Valois line was extinguished on Henry III's death in 1589, but he had to fight the Holy League, which was then in open rebellion, to claim the throne. His conversion to Catholicism in 1593 appeased many of the rebels, but some fought on until 1598. An assassin took his life in 1610.

Louis of Bourbon, prince of Condé (1530–1569)   An uncle of Henry of Navarre, he converted to Protestantism during the Habsburg wars and allowed himself to be named protector of the French Reformed churches. He led the Huguenots into war in 1562 and served the cause until slain on the battlefield in 1569.

Marguerite of Valois (1553–1615)   The daughter of Henry II and Catherine de Medici; her marriage to Henry of Navarre provided the occasion for the Saint Bartholomew's Day Massacre. The couple had effectively separated long before Henry came to the throne of France, so she was never crowned queen. A belated annulment allowed Henry to remarry in 1600.

PART TWO

The Documents

1

Religious Divisions in Sixteenth-Century France

Opposing Views of the True Faith

1

SIMON DU ROSIER

The Antithesis of Jesus Christ and the Pope

1561

The Antithesis of Jesus Christ and the Pope *instructs readers in Protestant doctrine through derogatory comparisons with Catholic teachings. Published in at least eight Latin and French editions, it enlarged on a German satire against Rome first published in 1521. The* Antithesis *pairs illustrations of the life of Jesus Christ with images depicting parallel situations in the lives of the popes. One pair, for example, contrasts an image of Christ washing the feet of his disciples with one of courtiers kissing the pope's feet, effectively contrasting Christ's humility with the worldly vanity of the popes. The scenes reproduced here are intended to teach the reader the true meaning of Christ's Last Supper and to*

Antithese des faicts de Jesus Christ et du Pape, Nouvellement mis en vers françois. Ensemble les commandemens du Pape, opposez aux commandemens de Dieu. Avec la description de l'image de l'Antichrist, selon l'Escriture sainte (n.p., 1561), 45–47, 46–48. Published anonymously, the book has been identified as the work of the Protestant minister Simon Du Rosier. By permission of Houghton Library, Harvard University.

denounce the misuse of this ceremony in the Catholic Mass. At issue is Catholics' belief that the priest's consecration of bread and wine in the Mass transforms these elements into the body and blood of Christ, thereby renewing the salvation promised at his death.

The illustration on the left-hand page depicts the Last Supper; that on the right depicts the pope celebrating Mass. The verses below the left-hand scene explain that Christ instituted the Lord's Supper in commemoration of his death, which washed his followers clean of sin, but warn that he never intended the equation between body and bread or blood and wine to be taken literally. The verses under the right-hand image more directly attack the Catholic teaching that, in giving his disciples bread and wine and telling them that they were his body and blood, Christ was giving them (and, by extension, priests of the church they founded) the power to replicate his own sacrifice on the Cross and thus to convey saving grace.

Why did Protestants believe that these theological differences were so essential that they left the Catholic Church on this account? And why, from the Catholic perspective, were these Protestant teachings not mere misunderstandings but heretical deviations that, if unsuppressed, threatened the very foundations of the church?

Verses explicating the left-hand image:

> Jesus, wanting the death he had taken on
> To be remembered in his faithful church,
> Gave the Lord's Supper to his chosen twelve
> And ordained it for all of us forever.
> Beginning thus this holy mystery,
> He took bread, gave thanks to God his Father,
> Then he broke it and, giving it to them, said:
> Take, eat. This is my body,
> Which for you has been given in sacrifice.
> After that he gave them the chalice,
> Saying to them, Drink of this all of you,
> For it is my blood which is shed for you.
> My blood, I say, of the New Testament,
> The perfect cleanser for your sins.
>   In this divine utterance of Jesus Christ,
> It is clear that he is not speaking
> Of bread and wine, but of his own body,

✠ IESVS CHRIST

Christ sa Cene nous institue,
Quand aux siens il l'a distribue.

Antithese XII.

IEsus voulant de la mort qu'il a prise
Laisser memoire en sa fidele Eglise,
Et à iamais pour nous tous ordonnée.
Commençant donc ce tant digne mystere,
Il print du pain, rend grace à Dieu son Pere:
Puis le rompit, leur baillant, dit ainsi:
Prenez, mangez. Le mien corps c'est cecy:
Qui pour vous est liuré en sacrifice.
Aprés cela leur bailla le calice

Mat 26.
Mar 14.
Luc 22.
1 Cor 11.

✠ E iij

LE PAPE

Contre la Cene de Iesus
Le Pape met la Messe sus.

Antithese XII.

IL y a moins d'accord & conuenance
Entre la Cene, & la fausse ordonnance
Qu'est de la Messe en la Papalité,
Qu'entre la nuit obscure & la clarté.
Veu que par tout nous enseigne la Bible,
Que Iesus Christ souffrant en corps paisible
Vn coup pour tous nous a remis en grace,
Et de son corps tant grande est l'efficace,
Que c'est le seul sacrifice asseuré
Pour noz pechez destruire demeuré.

D ij   ✠ Lis

Put on the Cross in torment and shame,
And of the blood distilled from his body,
For if he was speaking of bread and wine,
He would not have needed to suffer so much anguish.
　　Let us thus not think that the bread and wine
Are the body and blood of Christ, for he sits
At the right hand of God, where he will remain
Until the Judgment Day.
But let us take them, in making use of this sacrament,
As only a figure and sign,
Signifying to us the body of Jesus,
And also his blood, and testifying to us
That just as our bodies are nourished
With bread and wine, so also our spirits
With the body and blood of Christ, the celestial bread,
Are nourished, as the Holy Spirit
Of the Lord who is our only God
Attests and renders certain.
　　Receive thus the bread and wine as signs,
And seek Christ in his divine mansions
Of living faith; for then certainly
He will nourish us spiritually.

Verses explicating the right-hand image:

There is less agreement and conformity
Between the Lord's Supper and the false ordinance
That is the Mass in the papacy
Than between dark night and clarity of day.
Given that everywhere the Bible teaches us
That Jesus Christ, suffering in his tranquil body
One blow for all, restored us to grace,
And so great is the efficacity of his body
That it remains the only sure sacrifice
To destroy our sins.
　　Oh, is it not a blasphemous thing
To call the Mass a propitiatory act
And sacrifice agreeable to the Lord
Able to efface any sin?
　　Whoever believes that another offering is required

To wash away the sins committed
Than Jesus's body placed on the Cross
Is rejecting the voice of the Holy Spirit.
    Jesus put an end to all sacrifices
By his alone, and gave over himself
So that the virtue of his very worthy offering
Should be permanent, and any other annulled.
    Aside from this, there is nothing
That can take away the sins that ensnare us.
Thus one sees the arrogance of the pretenders[1]
Who claim to have this power
By means of the Antichrist, their head,
To offer up again Jesus's body.
For only Jesus has that function;
He has no successor who can
Repeat it. Besides, in establishing his supper
He did not command us to offer but rather to take
The bread and wine to eat and drink them,
While celebrating the memory of his name.
    Let us thus reject this putrid Mass,
Which is entirely contrary to the Lord's Supper
Keeping us from Jesus at the table,
At his sacred and delectable banquet:
In him alone let us seek our spiritual meat,
As he commands us.

---

[1] In French, *caphards*, meaning falsely devout and referring to Catholic priests.

2

ARTUS DESIRÉ

Description of the City of God Besieged by the Wretched Heretics

1550

In this treatise, Artus Desiré (ca. 1510–1579), one of the most prolific Catholic polemicists, calls on Catholics to contemplate the war that is being waged against the City of God by its carnal enemies. He first describes the City of God, which he equates with the Catholic Church, as resting on foundations of faith, with walls of chastity and a deep surrounding moat of humility. The gate through which one enters the city is the sacrament of baptism. Depicting the city as besieged from all sides by armies of heretics, Desiré calls on good Catholics to come to the city's defense. The argument is made graphically in the illustrations reproduced here. Employing a slander first used in ancient times, Desiré then goes on to denounce the heretics as sexual libertines who seduce others to join them in their debauchery. Why might people have found such a charge credible?

We will have accomplished nothing if we do not work still harder
To further reinforce the fortress,
And all Christians must work with us.
We need to raise a strong wall,
Which we will make out of full virginity,
To resist the carnality
Of the unfortunate and errant priapists,[1]
Who use this to seduce the papists,
And make them believe in their damnable errors.
The majority of these miserable people,

[1]Priapus was the Roman god of male sexuality.

[Artus Desiré], *Description de la Cité de Dieu figurée à nostre mere Saincte eglise, assiegée des malheureux heretiques qui se sont levez contre elles devers Midi, Orient, Occident, & Septrion. Avec l'assault des fidelles chrestiens appelez pour deffendre la dite cité* [Rouen, 1550], fol. 8v. Bibliothèque nationale de France.

La Cité de Dieu aſſiegée des Heretiques.

Such as apostates and renegade monks,
Carnal priests and the excommunicated,
Only left the Catholic Church
So as to live in debauchery
And follow their sensuality.
Every human being is assaulted
By this sin, which makes ceaseless war against us,
And, suddenly overtaken on earth,
Is dragged into the pits of the carnal enemy.
    Let us all pray to our eternal father
To preserve us from these lubricious assaults
And let us not do like the heretics
Who, to follow their carnal liberty,
Have renounced our paternal law,
To their great shame and damnation.
Preserve us well from their infection
And to this end let us be more firm
In resisting the warning calls
Of Satan, who tempts and assaults us.
We must fortify our city
With continence and virgin stone
To evict the infernal viper
Who attempts to destroy it.
Let us retreat into God
And gird ourselves with chastity
So as to have a strong defense
That neither devil, world, nor flesh,
Nor any other enemy will dare approach.

The Affair of the Rue Saint-Jacques

3

CLAUDE HATON

A Catholic View of Clandestine Protestant Services

1557

Claude Haton (b. 1534), a priest in the town of Provins, about forty miles southeast of Paris, describes the religious practices he attributed to French Protestants in the following passage from his memoirs. Haton did not begin to write his memoirs for some years after the events he describes, although he may have kept notebooks or journals that have since disappeared. This account necessarily reflects some hindsight, then, and is not a strictly contemporaneous view of events. It nevertheless shows a common Catholic understanding of the origins and character of the new religion. Like Artus Desiré (Document 2), Haton closely associates heresy with sexual debauchery. How is Haton's understanding of what occurred when Protestants met in the rue Saint-Jacques colored not only by these assumptions about debauchery but also by certain assumptions about gender and class?

One of the principal reasons for the aforementioned jubilee,[1] in addition to those already mentioned, was heresy, which was taking root in Christendom, in some provinces publicly, such as in the German and Swiss states, in other provinces secretly, as in Italy, Spain, France, and Navarre. The kingdoms of Scotland and England were already divided in two,

---

[1]In the Catholic Church, a jubilee was a time when Christians might gain special indulgences for performing specified acts of penitence and piety. The pope had called for a jubilee in 1557 to "appease the wrath of God," which was being manifest in epidemics, wars, and other scourges, among them heresy.

Claude Haton, *Mémoires contenant le récit des événements accomplis de 1553 à 1582*, ed. Félix Bourquelot (Paris, 1857), 1:48–53.

with one part heretics and the other Catholics. The French heretics, who were called Lutherans,[2] were striving greatly to enlarge their numbers and win over princes or great lords, in order to sustain and defend them in all ways and against all enemies. At the same time, their expansion and other strategies were worked out as secretly as possible out of fear of getting caught, for anyone caught was immediately thrown into jail, tried, and sentenced to be burned to death. Seldom did a month go by without a burning in Paris and two or three in Meaux and Troyes in Champagne, and in some months there were more than a dozen. And yet despite this, the others did not cease to pursue their enterprise of putting forward their false religion, and through their efforts managed to seduce a large number of persons of all sorts, including bishops, abbots, priors, monks, and priests, as well as laymen and laywomen, both nobles and commoners, small and great. And the means that they found most useful for bringing in large numbers and attracting so many clerics of all sorts was the generosity with which they offered their belongings and bodies to those who wished to follow them, and principally to monks and churchmen, to whom the men of this false Lutheran religion gave and abandoned their wives to take carnal pleasure with and their belongings to live from. And they were taught to do this by their ministers and preachers, who were all apostate priests and monks who had been enticed away from the true religion. This carnal liberty, which the heretic Lutherans called "fraternal charity," corrupted several ecclesiastics of various sorts and caused them to follow the aforesaid heretics. Most followed them only on account of this carnal and voluptuous charity. Those who had had their fill broke with them; the others remained and married women whom they then loaned to others, as had been done for them. And these heretic Lutherans were not even ashamed to be known as cuckolds, seeing as how their wives lent and abandoned themselves to win over men who wished to follow their false religion.

For this purpose, these Lutherans often held secret assemblies day and night in which they sermonized one another, both inside and outside of cities, in one of their members' houses, so as, they said, to serve the Lord and praise him. One of them would read some chapter of the Old or New Testament from a Bible written or printed in French

[2]The term *Lutheran* was applied indiscriminately to all Protestants until at least 1560.

which seemed to him suitable for the pleasure of the assembly.[3] . . . And to move their own hearts and those of their new brothers, they would sing two or three psalms of David translated into rhymed French by [the poet] Clément Marot and later set to music. . . . Once this was completed, it was permitted for men to approach the women and women the men, each as their pleasure led them; and after they had greeted and expressed affection for one another, the minister or preacher who was in charge would announce the charity of body and goods that they owed one another so as to belong to that religion, and, blowing out and extinguishing the candles before him, he would say words such as these: "In the name of God, accomplish the fraternal charity, each of you enjoying what he or she likes best." This being said and done, each would accommodate the other and satisfy their desires.

It is worth noting that during this time, a number of women in French cities and princes and gentlemen of the country, even at court and among the king's attendants, were beguiled by that Lutheran religion. These women, in order to attend the assemblies, would steal away from their husbands, who were totally unsuspecting because they remained Catholics. Some were accompanied by their chambermaids, others by their own daughters, so as to avoid awakening their husbands' suspicions when they went to the aforesaid secret assemblies, which took place largely at night and during the evening. Most, when they first went, were chaste wives and girls, but on their return were whores and sluts on account of the charity. At the beginning, in the city of Paris and elsewhere, the Lutherans assembled only once or twice a month and principally at night, for fear of being surprised and discovered, but then they began to go out of the city in the daytime, under the pretext of going out for a walk together in the country, so as to give themselves over more freely to their pleasures and the satisfaction of their desires. Still, after some time, they found their numbers strong enough and sufficiently protected by great lords and ladies to undertake to assemble more often at night, principally within the city of Paris, where they held their assemblies first in one quarter of the city and then in another, so as not to be easily discovered. And for

[3]Protestants encouraged the translation of the Bible into vernacular languages so that people could read scripture for themselves. Catholic authorities insisted that it be kept in Latin because they believed the Bible too difficult and easily misunderstood for laypeople to read it themselves.

some time, no one took notice of them, as they locked themselves up in the house where the assembly was convoked. But because nothing can be done so secretly that it is not known at last, these Lutherans were discovered and fallen upon on several occasions; though sometimes because of their great numbers they could not all be arrested and other times only a few women remained, who, being useless, were permitted to leave after having charitably given satisfaction to two or three good fellows.

One of these times, during the current year, the king, who was in Paris, was advised of the Lutherans' nocturnal assemblies and gave orders to set watch in all the quarters of the city and especially near the houses where the Lutherans were accustomed to gather, without making any noise or seeming to keep watch over them, so that when they had assembled it would be possible to lay hands on them and make a public example of their punishment. Following the king's orders, such an effort was made that one night the aforesaid charitable Lutherans were found assembled in a house in the university quarter, in or near the rue Saint-Jacques, I believe, and the king, who was lodging in the Louvre,[4] was notified and sent his provost with several guardsmen and members of the Paris night watch, both on foot and on horseback, to take prisoner without exception all of these practitioners of charity. The aforesaid provost, guardsmen, and members of the night watch, following the king's orders, proceeded to invade the lodging where the charitable ones had assembled, who, finding themselves surprised, no longer desired to accomplish their fraternal charity but rather advised all of the brothers to flee, leaving their sisters in danger. Some climbed up the drain spouts and fled over the rooftops; others hid in the attics, cellars, and recesses in walls; still others threw themselves out the windows, some dying in the process, others breaking their legs or arms. In sum, those who were able to escape without being caught or recognized could consider themselves quite lucky. Once the lodging had been forced so as to effect entry, the ladies of charity were found, abandoned by their charitable accomplices and completely dumbfounded by the embarrassment of being recognized. Those who were most noble hoped to escape with their faces veiled and hidden, but the officers did not permit this. The officers were astounded when they recognized some of the ladies, who were believed to be among the greatest in the kingdom and of almost royal blood, and whom they allowed to return

[4]At this time, the Louvre was the royal palace where the king usually resided while in Paris.

home in whatever company pleased them and without other proceedings. These [ladies] wanted and indeed demanded that the provost abandon his enterprise without taking any prisoners, but he did not dare to do this, for fear of the king's reproach. He nevertheless allowed the other ladies to leave as well, as a favor to them and on account of their social standing, and took prisoner only a large number of men, most of whom were priests, monks, Franciscans, Dominicans, and other clerics, who were taken to various prisons, . . . which were so full that no room remained in them. And yet very little punishment was handed out. Some were publicly whipped through the streets, others sent to the galleys, and still others banished from the kingdom, so as to conceal from the king the involvement of the aforementioned persons of high standing, who intervened in favor of the other prisoners. In this way, the secret of the Lutherans and their ladies was disclosed by several persons of both sexes, who declared to their judges that the only reason they attended this assembly was the carnal pleasure they took with one another, after which they no longer wished to follow the aforesaid Lutheran religion and abandoned it as a wicked thing.

4

REFORMED CHURCH OF PARIS

Report to the Swiss Delegation concerning the Affair of the Rue Saint-Jacques
1557

When Protestant leaders in Switzerland learned that a good number of French Protestants had been imprisoned for participating in religious services in Paris, they dispatched ambassadors from four key cities— Zurich, Bern, Basel, and Schaffhausen—to intervene on behalf of their coreligionists. At the same time, they requested further information from the leaders of the French Reformed church, so as to be better informed

Fernand Aubert, "À propos de l'affaire de la rue Saint-Jacques (4–5 septembre 1557). Un rapport présenté par l'Église de Paris à la délégation helvétique, *Bulletin de la Société de l'histoire du Protestantisme français 96* (1947): 96–102.

when they presented their case to the king. This is the report the French church sent them. How does this report differ from Claude Haton's account (Document 3), not just in its basic narrative of events but also in its representation of both the role played by women and the social profile of Paris's Protestant church?

Magnificent Lords,

Happy to comply with your desire to better acquaint yourselves with the events to which you intend to attract the attention of our king, we present you with a brief account of the sensations we experienced and the ferocity of the enemies of Christ. You will be particularly edified by the manner in which [these enemies] determined to ruin our unfortunate church. You will then be able to oppose the outrages committed by those who calumny us in the eyes of our sovereign.

About two years ago, God caused the seeds of the true church (as all of yours are) to sprout in the sight and knowledge, so to speak, of all of France. We learned little by little how much God approved of these beginnings despite their paltriness and great weakness. Indeed, in very little time, he made the church progress to such a point that Christ's harvest appeared nowhere more abundant. For the crowd that gathered in our assemblies included not only common people with little education but also—in appreciable numbers—the French elite, including many nobles and magistrates; in brief, all those whom papism had begun to disgust. Our meetings were only disdained by those whom Catholic ceremonies dazzled to the point of blindness, or who closed their eyes in order to feast on their rich religious benefices. Until now, then, in all conscientiousness and with an extraordinary desire to enlarge the kingdom of God, we have enjoyed this inestimable help from on high. For during all of this time, Providence has protected us—we who were in the very mouth of lions avid to gorge on our blood. We are confident that it will continue to be so.

Thus it was that on September 5, when some four hundred of us were gathered for Communion, several priests, accompanied by others out of the same swamp, invaded and observed us. The next morning at daybreak, as everyone was returning home, we suddenly met with a hail of stones. Armed commoners of the most wretched sort attacked unarmed [worshippers] and tried to commit all sorts of cruelties against us. They doubtless thought to accomplish a brilliant exploit in obliterating or throwing into prison some Lutherans, heretics, brigands, assassins—such are the slanders they heaped upon us. They accused us, in effect, of all sorts of wickedness, such as sieges and wars. Should we mention the rumors that spread through the city that we had assembled for abominable debauchery? In the opinion of some, to give ourselves over to drunken orgies and gluttony. According to others, to attack the Sorbonnists' school, and so forth. The most false rumors, the most unbelievable, and the most disgusting were avidly taken up by our adversaries.

But the outrages were not only verbal, as about 130 of our own could not, or would not, try to escape the bestial violence of the populace. They were tied up like enemies by these rogues and stripped of their money, jewelry, and other objects of value. Honorable women and girls from the best families had their headdresses insolently pulled off, their garments torn. Everyone's face, regardless of sex, class, or age, was streaked with mud. Strengthened by the complicity and even approval of the judges, the most rash and wicked were congratulated above all, such that anyone endowed with some human sentiment could easily see that all of these people conspired with one and the same impetus against the children of God.

At first we were not able to approach our brothers enclosed in a black prison to console them and aid them in their distress. If we solicited a meeting with them, we were immediately charged with heresy—a difficult suspicion to avoid. And it wasn't one unique Cerberus, but several intractable ones, who stood before us. Their insurmountable hatred for holy doctrine obliged us to renounce visiting our brothers. From this they suffered greatly, and still do.

While the faithful were treated in a cruel and horrible fashion in prison, the king chose twenty judges, animated above all by an ardent hatred for our doctrine, and who, less well educated than the others, greatly surpassed them in cruelty. Invested with a specific charge, they first gave three of our number over to be burned at the stake for the sole reason that (in their own words) they had "abandoned the customs of their ancestors." These judges did not refer to any scriptural authority; what is more, confounded by numerous citations, they replied only with threats. They continually urged [the prisoners] to recant or suffer the penalty of being burned to death. The three faithful responded that they were ready to retract their beliefs if they were convinced by the evidence of scripture. As they persisted in that attitude, they were publicly burned on September 26, after having their tongues cut out. Two of them were elders of our church, of a remarkable piety and moral purity. They were joined by a woman truly noble by birth and spirit who, animated by an extraordinary ardor, allowed herself to be taken to the site of the execution, where she submitted to a cruel martyrdom with a firmness equal to the serenity of her expression. Two others courageously offered the Lord a like agony on October 2. It was the same on October 23 for two beardless youths—one only eighteen, the other scarcely older—endowed with the same sentiments and the same fidelity. Strangled and then burned, they evoked pity even from papists, shamed to see adolescents, on whose face one could easily read an honest nature and candid heart, tortured with such cruel savagery.

Such is the ferocity these people use with regard to our brothers.

Now they menace us with still worse things if God, by your intervention or by other means, does not put a stop to their audacity and their cruelty.

Such is the ineptitude of those to whom our king has confided the task of pronouncing judgment on us that they attach no more importance to the Word of God than to a profane text, and much less than to the decrees of the popes and inventions of their disciples. Given the eminence of your learning, your authority will permit you to demonstrate without difficulty to our sovereign how far they have strayed from the true end and that they are inundated with darkness instead of light.

There, perfectly narrated, are the essentials of the things that are, in our opinion, proper to tell the king in order to attend in some measure to the tranquillity of our church. In your wisdom, you may add or omit what seems fitting to you.

By Jesus Christ our mediator, we ask God to give a happy outcome to your embassy, to safeguard always your authority, and to abundantly crown you with his grace.

Persecution and Conversion

5

PARLEMENT OF PARIS

Conviction of Marguerite Le Riche for Heresy
August 19, 1559

The following judgment was handed down by the Parlement (high court) of Paris in August 1559, during the brief period following the death of Henry II, when the influence of Francis, duke of Guise, and Charles, cardinal of Lorraine, over the young king Francis II caused an increase in prosecutions for heresy. The sentence follows the format common to all of the court's judgments; it summarizes the various stages of the prisoner's prosecution (while remaining maddeningly elusive about the actual crimes for which she has been judged guilty) and then sets out the prescribed punishment. As the judgment shows, accused heretics were given several opportunities to recant their errors before being convicted of heresy. Only those who repeatedly refused to recant were sentenced to death for the crime. When torture was ordered, as it was in this case, its purpose was to elicit information that might lead to more arrests and not merely to obtain a confession of heretical beliefs or practices.

The court, having seen the criminal proceedings executed by the examining magistrates appointed by the court for this case and by the bishop of Paris or his official following the ruling given by the court on last May 5, on the request and proceedings instituted by the king's attorney general, serving as plaintiff for the crime of heresy charged against Marguerite Le Riche, wife of Antoine Ricault, a merchant bookseller living on the mont Saint-Hillaire in Paris at the sign of the Giant Quail, prisoner in the Conciergerie,[1] defendant in the case. Seen also: the sentence handed down by the bishop's official against the aforesaid

---

[1]The Paris prison where accused heretics awaited trial and sentencing.

Archives nationales de France (Paris), Criminal register X^{2a} 124 (August 19, 1559).

Marguerite Le Riche, by which he handed her over to the secular arm and discharged her to the custody of the prisons of the Conciergerie,[2] and the conclusions drawn by the king's attorney general. The prisoner having been heard and interrogated by the court on the crimes and infractions fully described in the proceedings. And after the prisoner was admonished on several different occasions, consistent with the court's ruling, both by former doctors of the faculty of theology and by other upstanding and notable persons, and nevertheless persisted in the aforesaid heretical blasphemies. All things considered.

It shall be pronounced that the court, on account of the scandalous, heretical, and sacramentarian blasphemies uttered by the prisoner against the honor of God, the Blessed Sacrament of the altar, and other sacraments of our Holy Mother Church, and its constitutions and commandments fully described in the proceedings, has condemned and condemns the prisoner, Marguerite Le Riche, to be taken in a cart from the prisons of the Conciergerie to the place Maubert and to be suspended from a gallows erected there, around which shall be built a fire in which her body shall be set aflame, burned, consumed, and reduced to ashes. And [the court] has declared and declares all of her belongings forfeited to the king to be employed in alms and other charitable works, following the king's edict. The court nevertheless orders that before the execution of Marguerite Le Riche she shall be tortured and stretched on the rack to make her declare and name those who were her accomplices and supporters in the aforesaid crimes and also the location of the house in the faubourg of Saint-Victor where she went [for services] last Easter. This shall be done according to the customary procedures.

[The judgment is followed by an order requiring Le Riche to be visited by two midwives to be certain she is not pregnant before carrying out the sentence. It is further specified that only the sentence of torture shall be read to her, and not the death sentence, until after the torture has been carried out. Finally, the appended order adds that she is to be strangled before she feels the flames, but that if she persists in her blasphemies, she is to be gagged before leaving the prison. These last clauses are revealing. By ordering her strangled, the judges quietly tempered the cruel death of

---

[2]The church had traditionally judged heresy cases and then passed convicted heretics to secular authorities for punishment. Kings Francis I and Henry II had shifted this responsibility to secular courts so as to reduce delays, but church officials still investigated heresy charges, too.

being burned alive. At the same time, they did not want to risk a public profession of faith from the gallows that might have been received sympathetically by members of the attending crowd.]

6

JEAN PERRISSIN AND JACQUES TORTOREL

Anne du Bourg, Counselor in the Parlement of Paris, Burned on the Place de Grève

December 21, 1559

The most famous victim of the intensified attack on heresy during the reign of Francis II was a young counselor in the Parlement of Paris named Anne du Bourg. Du Bourg had caught the eye of Henry II in June 1559, when he defended "Lutheran" ideas at a special plenary session of the Parlement held in the king's presence. Angered by du Bourg's outspokenness, Henry ordered him arrested and was later heard to remark that he would see him burn with his own eyes. Henry did not see du Bourg burn. Pierced in the eye by his opponent's broken lance in a tournament a month after ordering the magistrate's arrest, the king died from the subsequent infection. Protestants were quick to see this as a judgment of God, but this did not keep the court from proceeding with the case. In December, du Bourg was sentenced to be executed publicly on the square in front of the Paris City Hall.

The woodcut reproduced here comes from a series of forty prints published in Geneva in 1569–1570 and illustrated by two artists from Lyons, Jean Perrissin and Jacques Tortorel. Scholars have shown that the artists carefully researched the events they portrayed in both published and unpublished sources and that the prints, sold separately and

Jean Perrissin and Jacques Tortorel, *Premier volume, contenant Quarante tableaux ou histoires diverses qui sont memorables touchant les guerres, massacres, et troubles advenues en France en ces dernieres annees* [Geneva, ca. 1570], as reproduced in Alfred Franklin, *Les grandes scènes historiques du XVIe siècle; reproduction fac-similé du recueil de J. Tortorel et J. Perrissin* (Paris, 1886), plate 5. Widener Library, Harvard College Library, H 1708.86PF.

Anne du Bourg Conseiller du Parlement de Paris bruslé a S. Iean en Greue le 21. Decembre. 1559.

Anne du Bourg ayant esté mené sur vne charrette en la place
Sainct Iean en Greue à Paris: & estant luy mesme despouillé, tel
qu'à la chemise: il guindé en vne potence, là où il est estranglé,
& puis son corps ietté au feu.

as sets, were widely distributed in France, the Netherlands, the Rhineland, and northern Germany.[1] *The prints are not overtly propagandistic and illustrate Protestant attacks on Catholics, as well as the reverse, along with battles won by each side in the civil wars. But was the artist responsible for this scene truly a neutral observer of events, or are there indications here of his personal religious sympathies?*

[1] See Philip Benedict, *Graphic History: The Wars, Massacres and Troubles of Tortorel and Perrissin* (Geneva: Droz, 2007), and Philip Benedict, Lawrence M. Bryant, and Kristen B. Neuschel, "Graphic History: What Readers Knew and Were Taught in the *Quarante Tableaux* of Perrissin and Tortorel," *French Historical Studies* 28 (Spring 2005): 175–229.

7

CHARLOTTE D'ARBALESTE

The Conversion of Jean de Pas, Lord of Feuquères

The tension between religious truth and worldly success is particularly evident in accounts of the conversion of aristocrats, for although all Reformed converts had to face up to the possibility of ultimately being convicted and executed for heresy, this was a fairly distant prospect — in proportion to France's Protestant population, the number of executions was not all that large — while the danger of losing the advantages that came from royal favor was immediate and very real. This tension is explicit in Charlotte d'Arbaleste's account of the conversion to Protestantism of her first husband, Jean de Pas, seigneur (lord) of Feuquères, in the memoir she later composed for her children.

In the passage immediately preceding this excerpt, Arbaleste explains that Feuquères was brought up as a page in the court of King Francis I's son Charles, duke of Orléans, until the latter's death in 1545. He subsequently served the king himself and the future king, Francis II, who, though just a child, developed a special affection for him and insisted on

Charlotte d'Arbaleste, *Mémoires de Madame de Mornay*, ed. Madame de Witt (Paris, 1868), 50–52.

keeping him at his side. While still quite young, Feuquères was given command of a company of light horse and made governor of Roye, a town on France's northern border, where he took part in the war between France and Spain. It was there that he had his first exposure to Protestant preaching.

There, he often heard a Franciscan who, despite his monk's habit, preached the truth. He was immediately attracted and began to recognize the abuses of the Roman church. Later, when he was in Italy with Monsieur de Guise, the French officers who accompanied Guise paid homage to the pope and kissed his slipper. He also noticed that, for a small sum of money paid to the pope, people were free to eat meat in Lent and on other forbidden days, while everywhere else, by the pope's authority, a man might be burned to death for eating an egg. This occasioned a great debate within his conscience on account of the desire he had to learn more and seek the truth, while, at the same time, he saw himself advancing at court and on the point of receiving rewards and honors that he could never hope to achieve if he made profession of the truth, but rather, to the contrary, he would be banished from France, where the fires of persecution were already alight. I often heard him say that he became sick worrying about the choice he had to make. He finally resolved, on reading the Second Psalm, to forget all worldly considerations, recognizing that it was all too common for kings and princes to align themselves against God and Jesus Christ, his beloved king.[1] Thus, he resolved to leave the Mass and the abuses of the Catholic Church and to profess the truth; and yet he did not abandon the court, where often he and some other zealous converts were able to listen to Protestant sermons in the apartments of the queen mother while she was at dinner, with the help of her Protestant serving ladies.

[Like many converts, Feuquères initially adopted a moderate position, ceasing to attend Catholic ceremonies but trying not to provoke arrest by keeping his Protestant devotions secret. He finally had to choose sides when the first religious war broke out in 1562. He served in the Protestant army until his death as a result of battle injuries in 1569.]

---

[1] The verses to which he refers read: "Why are the nations in turmoil? Why do the peoples hatch their futile plots? Kings of the earth stand ready, and princes conspire together against the Lord and his anointed king" (Psalms 2:1–2).

Growing Religious Tensions

8

JEAN PERRISSIN AND JACQUES TORTOREL

The Massacre at Cahors in Quercy

November 19, 1561

By 1560, religious tensions were acute, especially in the south of France, where the Protestants were strongest and, as a consequence, boldest about committing acts of iconoclasm, seizing churches, and defying edicts forbidding public worship. This woodcut by Jacques Tortorel, from the same series as Document 6, illustrates events reported to have occurred in Cahors in November 1561. According to the unpublished account now in Genevan archives from which Tortorel appears to have reconstructed this scene, priests attached to the Cahors cathedral plotted this attack on a house where Protestants had gathered for worship. In all, forty-eight or fifty people were killed.[1]

The details identified in the caption are A (upper right), the house belonging to Monsieur de Cabreyret where people had assembled to hear a sermon; B (upper right and upper left), the fire set at three corners of the house; C (lower center), the main entry, where the attackers took the Protestants to kill them; D (bottom center), the twenty-five or thirty dead bodies laid out in the street; E (bottom left), the stream of blood flowing from the bodies; F (top center), the neighboring church whose priests had incited the trouble.

How does the scene shown here compare with Catholic accounts (Documents 3 and 9) of breaking up such meetings and the violence that

---

[1]Philip Benedict, Lawrence M. Bryant, and Kristen B. Neuschel, "Graphic History: What Readers Knew and Were Taught in the *Quarante Tableaux* of Perrissin and Tortorel," *French Historical Studies* 28 (Spring 2005): 102–3.

Jean Perrissin and Jacques Tortorel, *Premier volume, contenant Quarante tableaux ou histoires diverses qui sont memorables touchant les guerres, massacres, et troubles advenues en France en ces dernieres annees* [Geneva, ca. 1570], as reproduced in Alfred Franklin, *Les grandes scènes historiques du XVIe siècle; reproduction fac-similé du recueil de J. Tortorel et J. Perrissin* (Paris, 1886), plate 8. Bibliothèque nationale de France.

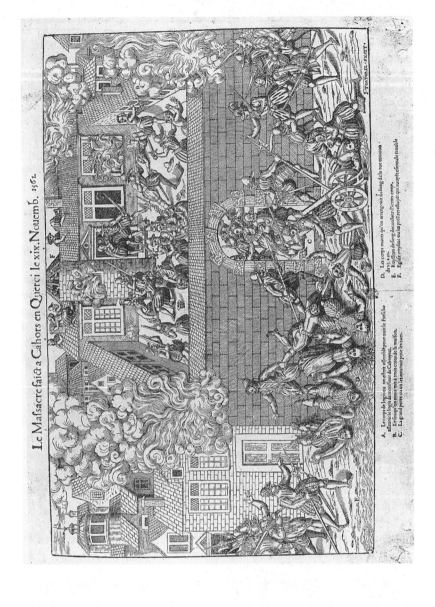

Le Maſſacre faict a Cahors en Querci le xix. Nouemb. 1561.

A. Le coup de piſtolet qu'on feit aſſembler pour ouïr le Preſche eſtant le logis de monſieur de Cabueyne.
B. Le lieu qu'on auoit mis à ruer coutre la maiſon.
C. La grad porte qu'on ſe cramoiſir pour le tuer.
D. Les corps morts qu'on a renpoict au long de la rue cinq ou ſix des 3, 4, 60.
E. Roideau de ſing decoulle au la ruem corp.
F. Eglise roydàr ou la pieſche de ligſe qui auoit eu rencule treuoible.

64

ensued? Are men and women being treated differently here? Why would the killers have bothered to lay out the dead in the street?

9

CLAUDE DE SAINCTES

Discourse on the Sacking of Catholic Churches by the Heretics

1562

In Paris, the most inflammatory episode of religious violence during the months that led up to the outbreak of civil war occurred when Protestants assembled for worship at a house outside the city walls, in the faubourg of Saint-Marcel, battled Catholics in the neighboring church of Saint-Médard. The following narrative of these events was written by a Catholic priest, Claude de Sainctes (1525–1591), and published in 1562 as part of a broader polemic recounting iconoclastic acts and pillaging of churches committed by religious dissenters in both ancient and modern times. Document 10 recounts the same riot from a Protestant point of view.

Around Christmas, a large number of people—many more than usual—gathered in Paris and went armed to hear [Protestant] preaching. Some days they met outside the Saint-Antoine gate in a place called Popincourt, other days in the faubourg of Saint-Marcel in the garden of a house called the Patriarch. It was easy to see that the gathering of so many people was done with some evil intent, for they were so insolent that no one dared to go near them in the street or even to look them in the eye. They brazenly attacked people, striking and menacing everyone without anyone daring to fight back, and just waiting for

Claude de Sainctes, *Discours sur le saccagement des eglises catholiques par les heretiques anciens et nouveaux Calvinistes de l'an Mil cinq cens soixante et deux* (Toulouse, 1562), fols. 31–33.

a chance to do the job for which they had been summoned, though still fearful of the great multitude of people, notwithstanding the fact that the population was disarmed, for any bourgeois citizen found with a sword, unless he was a Huguenot, would have been seized as seditious. And yet the conspirators were armed to the teeth. Two days after Christmas, on Saint John's Day, this great crowd of debauched people was attending services in the place called the Patriarch, and, since it was a holy day, the Catholics were ringing vespers after their sermon in the church of Saint-Médard, where people had assembled as usual.

The Huguenots took offense at the sound of the bells and claimed that they were interfering with God's Word, and without other provocation, they ran to sack this poor church [Saint-Médard], which had not yet even been completed. They broke down all the doors, entered with swords and pistols in hand, and struck without discretion, outraging the people, who were weaponless and had no thought of battle. Among others, they singled out the priest who had preached to the Catholics and furiously threw themselves upon him when he was on his knees so as to cut off his head. And in fact they slashed the collar of his robes and other garments and even cut his neck a bit, as they beat him at will and rained sword strokes upon him. They killed some parishioners and injured others. They broke up the Blessed Sacrament, threw it to the floor, and ground it under their feet. They did not spare the head of a single statue, as if they were living and feeling saints. They broke out most of the windows, broke up a number of altars, and stole the ornaments, chalices, relics, and generally all that they could carry. Gabaston, the watch commander, entered on horseback as far as the main altar and cried out in corrupt Gascon, "Pillage everything; pillage everything."[1] They boasted of having defecated in the baptismal font, and whoever among them could say or do the worst was the most esteemed. I leave to each reader to judge the tears, outcries, and expressions of these good people of Paris, so faithful to God and

---

[1] As the watch commander, or head of the troops charged with maintaining order in Paris, Gabaston was supposed to put an end to the riots, but this and other Catholic accounts accuse him instead of allying himself and his troops with the Protestants. Gabaston's Gascon accent, which identified him as coming from a part of France where Protestantism was strongest, only added to the suspicions against him. An inquest of the Parlement of Paris, held by order of the crown, initially deadlocked over contradictory evidence but ultimately made a scapegoat out of Gabaston, blaming him for arresting only Catholics and for not having prevented the pillaging of Saint-Médard. He was sentenced to death and hanged on the place de Grève, in front of the City Hall, but the crowds snatched his body from the executioner, dragged it through the streets, and threw it into the Seine.

king, who witnessed priests and other men and women, bloody and injured, being dragged off to prison, tied together two by two like galley prisoners. They were then thrown into the bottom of a pit, with no compassion for their wounds or innocence, and some of them died there for lack of help.

No one would have dared to moan or sigh at such a spectacle. The watch commander and his men, paid by the Parisian bourgeoisie, protected the Huguenots and treated the Catholics like dogs. If someone raised his eyes, he was beaten and clubbed as a rioter. One poor woman was dragged by the hair into the gutter and beaten black-and-blue for simply having said while weeping, "What a great pity; will we always be so afflicted?" The Huguenots marched through the city in battle order, swords brazenly in hand and crying aloud, "The Gospel, the Gospel; where are the idolatrous papists?" and other blasphemous things. The people didn't know where to turn or to whom they should complain; those who should have protected them called them a mutinous and seditious people, and one they would soon soften up.

10

The True Story of the Insurrection, Uprising, and Sedition Directed by the Priests of Saint-Médard against the Faithful

1562

Protestant narratives of the Saint-Médard riots tell a very different story from the one told in Document 9. Neither the author nor the date of publication of the following account are known for certain, but it appears to have been published in defense of the Protestant cause shortly after the events in question. How did the authors of this and the previous account of the riot slant their stories so as to place their coreligionists in the right? Can a plausible narrative be pieced together from the two accounts in spite of omissions and contradictions?

Histoire véritable de la mutinerie, tumulte, et sédition faicte par les prestres de Sainct-Médard, le samedy 27 décembre 1561, as reproduced in *Archives curieuses de l'histoire de la France*, ed. Louis Lafaist (pseud. L. Cimber) and Félix Danjou, 1st series, vol. 4 (Paris, 1835), 52–56.

In 1561, on the Saturday after Christmas, the feast of Saint John, the 27th of December, the faithful were publicly assembled, as was permitted, in the suburb of Saint-Marcel in a place called the Patriarch. After prayers and the singing of a psalm, the minister, Monsieur Malot, began to preach on this passage from Saint Matthew, "Come to me, all you that labor and are heavy laden," which he had chosen as a source of sound doctrine and edification from which the audience (which was larger than usual on account of the holiday) might derive great fruit. After he had spoken for about a quarter of an hour, those of Saint-Médard, the suburb's parish church, began to ring all of their bells at the same time with deliberate malice, causing such a din that, inasmuch as there was only an alley separating the Patriarch from the church, it was completely impossible to hear the sermon. At this, the assembled group sent two unarmed men to beg them to cease ringing the bells, so that those gathered were not prevented from hearing the Word of God. Against this prayer and humble request, the voice of priests and other rogues was raised, crying that they would ring to spite them, at which point they began to try to create an even greater din with their bells. At the same time, they rebelliously slammed the main door to their church, shutting inside one of the emissaries. The other barely escaped and returned to his companions. As the one who remained had only a little knife on him, they slew him with seven blows from both pikes and swords, almost all of which were mortal wounds in the opinion of surgeons. They closed two other doors, a large one from the presbytery[1] and a small one to the cemetery, issuing onto the alley adjoining the Patriarch, and began to throw stones and shoot crossbow arrows, of which they had a large supply. The cry of those needing help alarmed the entire company, who until that point had no inkling of a riot and were greatly frightened and perplexed. And yet the priests only redoubled the clamor of their tocsin.[2]

Indeed, the three doors were closed, the rain of stones and missiles begun, and the tocsin sounded all so suddenly that it can only be imagined that people were at the ready in all of these places even before the call to cease ringing the bells. Nevertheless, despite these sudden and unexpected things, the evangelicals restored order in their assembly. After first drawing out of the assembly all of the men capable of defending it, which was very few by comparison with the great crowd outside (in my opinion, no less than twelve or thirteen

---

[1]The part of the church reserved for the officiating clergy.
[2]Alarm; the ringing of an alarm bell.

thousand persons), they reassured the others so well that after a psalm was sung, the sermon continued. However, the tocsin continued still to ring, alongside a furious deluge of stones and arrows. It so happened that within the assembly was the head of the mounted police force,[3] Monsieur Rougeoreille, who had been commissioned by the governor of Paris to guard the assembly, and he had with him five or six of his archers, one of whom he sent to speak to the parish priest and forbid him in the king's name to sound the tocsin and throw stones. Then he wanted to go himself, but the hail of stones and crossbow arrows forced him quickly to retreat, without any other response.

It was this refusal and rebellion against a magistrate that prompted the evangelicals, clearly recognizing the dangers their entire company faced, not to allow themselves to be pushed about any longer by these scarecrows and rabble-rousers. And thus it was that, armed more with good hearts and ardent zeal . . . than with [actual weapons], they all, with a singular courage, made such a great effort that they broke in the doors of the church. This was not accomplished without several men being injured, which increased their anger. They were further incited to vengeance by the compassion that overtook them when they found on the sill of the church their poor brother, who had been so outrageously beaten and killed. In this first fury appeared a number of priests and other troublemakers armed with swords, shields, pikes, paving stones, and crossbows, fighting to the utmost and with fierce resistance, but this lasted only a short time against the courageous effort of the others, such that they [the Catholics] were afterward overcome by fear and a large number of them escaped into the bell tower, cowardly abandoning their flock, which they had exposed to such slaughter. Among other clerics was the parish priest, the head and leader of the rebellion, who climbed to the top of the bell tower, from which he and his accomplices did not cease to attack the evangelicals for as long as the munitions, which they had long ago assembled, lasted. I cannot pass over in silence the prodigious fury of certain priests who were inflamed with such rage that when the mass of stones gathered in the church gave out, they climbed on the altars and with their own hands broke up the images that they had previously so reverently adored and threw pieces of them at their enemies—something that is nevertheless less remarkable than it may at first seem, given that this fury was inherent in their nature, for it would be hard to

---

[3]The *prévôt des maréschaux* headed the troops whose usual responsibility was keeping order in the countryside and on the roads.

judge whether they were more furious and maniacal when they thus irreligiously broke something they so honored or when they adored such inanimate things.

In this conflict, which lasted a good half hour, about thirty or forty rogues were injured and fourteen or fifteen of the principal leaders were taken prisoner. Several escaped, on account of the temerity of the seditious populace. . . . And all this time, those who had taken refuge in the bell tower, the leader of whom was the parish priest, persisted in ringing the tocsin, in hope of getting other troublemakers to come cut to pieces the innocent flock who persisted in hearing the Word of God. And there was no other way to make them stop, given the confidence they had in the fortress of their bell tower, than to threaten to burn it down. In this way, the rioting was brought to an end.

2

Religious War and the Intensification of Religious Hatreds, 1562–1570

11

Song on the Massacre of Vassy
1562

In a culture in which the large majority of the population was illiterate, songs sung in public venues such as inns and taverns remained an important means of communicating news and stirring up popular opinion. This song celebrates the brutal attack that troops serving Francis, duke of Guise, made on a group of Protestants gathered for worship in a barn outside the town of Vassy, east of Paris, on March 1, 1562.

By most accounts, the attack was not premeditated. The duke, stopping for Mass in the town church on his way to Paris with his family, was angered to learn that some five hundred people had assembled for Protestant services in a nearby barn and sent soldiers to order them to disperse. Greeted roughly and promptly evicted, the soldiers responded by gathering troops to attack the Protestant worshippers, who barricaded themselves in the barn and gathered a supply of stones to rain down on the returning soldiers. Stones, however, were a paltry defense against the guns of the duke's troops, and by the end of the day, some twenty-three worshippers were dead and more than a hundred wounded.[1] *Ignoring the*

[1] Like most facts concerning the Massacre of Vassy, the number of dead is subject to dispute. The figures given here are taken from Jean-Hippolyte Mariéjol, *La Réforme, la Ligue, L'Edit de Nantes, 1559–1598* (Paris: Taillandier, 1983), 74–75. Also in dispute is the question of whether the barn, which apparently abutted the walls of Vassy, technically lay outside them, in which case Protestant worship was legal according to the Edict of January 1562, or whether this worship was nevertheless forbidden because Vassy was a walled town.

Antoine-Jean-Victor Le Roux de Lincy, *Recueil de chants historiques français depuis le XIIᵉ jusqu'au XVIIIᵉ siècle* (Paris, 1841–1842), 2:269–72.

Protestant outcry, the duke proceeded on to Paris, where city leaders and residents alike gave him a hero's welcome.

The Protestant leader Louis of Bourbon, prince of Condé, in Paris to demand redress for the Massacre of Vassy, after sizing up the situation retreated to Orléans, summoned his troops, and prepared for war.

Honor be to God and to the king our lord,
Who protects us from the wrath of malicious Huguenots.
They want to kill us, but a day will come
When they will be made to die laughing.

We have a good lord in this country of France,
And a prince of great honor; valiant and humane.
He is the duke of Guise, who, by his great mercy,
Defended the Holy Mother Church at Vassy.

Sunday, March first, Huguenots came from all around
To gather in a barn for preaching and feasting
On meat and fat lard, like so many rats,
Though it was a time for Lenten fasting.

And when the good prince of Guise went to hear a Mass,
And the priest his vestments was donning,
The Huguenots, ignoble toads, rang the bells for worship,
Preventing God's service in the Holy Mother Church.

And so Monsieur de Guise said to his gentlemen:
Go over there and tell them to have patience,
Give us a moment's peace, so to render God
Grace, honor, and reverence.

But the cursed Huguenots did something else instead
And replied that they did not have to stop;
They struck and molested these noble persons;
With cannons and sticks they attacked them basely.

Monsieur de Guise went over there in haste,
And on those wicked ones took vengeance;
He killed most of their party, and his troops
By their conquests did something great.

12

FRANÇOIS GRIN

A Catholic View of the Surprise of Meaux
1567

The first War of Religion ended in March 1563 with a compromise peace that left both sides dissatisfied. Protestant leaders, convinced that the king was just waiting for a good chance to attack them, provoked the second war by deciding to strike first. The journal left by François Grin (ca. 1536–1611), a monk in Paris's ancient abbey of Saint-Victor, shows how Catholics interpreted this Huguenot offensive.

Friday, September 26, 1567, the town of Montereaux-sur-Yonne was taken by some disturbers of the public peace, otherwise known as Huguenots.

The following Saturday, the 27th, by the same persons and their accomplices, the city of Soissons was taken by surprise at four in the morning, during which [events] there were several massacres, churches and abbeys pillaged, and clerics murdered and killed.

The same day, at four or five in the evening, the town of Lagny-sur-Marne was similarly taken by the same conspirators, under the leadership of Monsieur Dharles, the abbot of the city's abbey and a great Huguenot. During the taking of the city, several citizens of Lagny were killed, among them clerics and monks from the abbey, and the abbey was ruined.

Sunday, the 28th, at three or four in the afternoon, the city of Orléans was taken by treachery by citizens of the city itself who were rebels and conspirators and enemies of God, the king, and the public peace. They afterward sacked and destroyed and pulled down all of the churches and abbeys in the city, like godless, kingless, and lawless madmen on whom the wrath of God will justly fall one day.

"Journal de François Grin, religieux de Saint Victor (1554–1570)," ed. Baron Alphonse de Ruble, *Mémoires de la Société de l'histoire de Paris et de l'Ile-de-France* 21 (1894): 40–42.

That same day, the king, having stopped at Meaux on his way back from visiting Picardy and preparing to celebrate Saint Michael's Day, was advised that some men, wishing him ill, were plotting to capture him by surprise—a thoroughly iniquitous and unheard-of thing—with the result that he hastened to Paris to be in greater security. Nevertheless, these frenzied madmen, thirsting for royal and human blood, attempted several ambushes. If it had not been for God's grace and power, along with the good order that prevailed because the king was accompanied by a number of nobles and four thousand or six thousand soldiers, the wretches would have succeeded in their damnable plot, which by God's mercy, they were unable to do. And the king arrived the same day in Paris, very frightened and rightly so. . . .

On Wednesday, the first of October 1567, the [Huguenots], full of rage and fury at having failed in their plan to take the king and kill him and then seize the crown, as has since been made evident, came very close to Paris, outside the Saint-Denis gate. They set fire to fifteen or sixteen windmills, which stunned the city, for they were trying to starve it out, but Our Lord, who always cares for his own, brought another outcome to these events and prevented the wicked plot from succeeding.

On Thursday, October 2, the [Huguenots], not content with these wretched and accursed acts, surprised the town of Saint-Denis at nine or ten in the morning. They occupied the city for six weeks, while awaiting the arrival of reinforcements, so as to ruin the king and the kingdom if they could. In the meantime, they raided and sacked nearby villages and hamlets, pillaging and destroying all of the churches, both in the aforesaid town of Saint-Denis and in neighboring villages—a more than barbarous and utterly iniquitous thing, being entirely godless and irrational.

13

CLAUDE HATON

The Execution in Effigy of Gaspard de Coligny
1569

In the summer of 1569, during the third War of Religion, the Parlement of Paris tried the Protestant leader Admiral Gaspard de Coligny in absentia, so that his extensive properties could be confiscated to the profit of a penurious crown. Claude Haton left the following account of the trial and subsequent execution in effigy of Coligny. (Internal evidence suggests that this passage was composed sometime between August 1570, when the Peace of Saint-Germain was announced, and September 1571, when Coligny returned to court.) Haton begins by quoting verbatim the Parlement's judgment against the admiral and then goes on to recount attempts that were rumored to have been made to collect the reward that the king promised to anyone who could deliver Coligny to him dead or alive. The document is especially interesting on two counts: first, because the acts carried out against the straw effigy in 1569 very closely resemble the punishments to which the admiral's real body was subjected on Saint Bartholomew's Day; second, because the man explicitly mentioned as hoping to collect the reward for capturing Coligny was the man commonly believed to have attempted to assassinate him on August 22, 1572, in the incident that touched off the Saint Bartholomew's Day Massacre.

"The Parlement of Paris having reviewed the proceedings against Gaspard de Coligny, the so-called admiral of France and lord of Chastillon-sur-Loing, including the evidence against him, the conclusions of the king's attorney general, and his noncompliance with the summons to appear, the aforesaid court declares him guilty of the crime of lese majesty[1] against God and the king, retracts his titles of nobility, and declares him and his children non-noble and commoners

[1]Treason.

Claude Haton, *Mémoires contenant le récit des événements accomplis de 1553 à 1582,* ed. Félix Bourquelot (Paris, 1857), vol. 2: 565–67.

forever. The court further orders that his coat of arms be dragged through the streets of Paris tied to the tail of a horse and that his body be dragged on a pallet through the streets of Paris from the Parlement's prison to the place de Grève, where it is to be hanged from a gallows and strangled until dead, and his estates, properties, castles, and houses, along with all of his revenues, confiscated to the profit of the king our lord."

The sentence was carried out not on his person, but in effigy. A straw man was made and dressed in the colors the admiral usually wore, with a face painted to resemble his portrait. It was brought out of the prisons of the Conciergerie and put on a pallet, which was harnessed to a horse to drag, while another horse had [the admiral's] coat of arms attached to its tail. The effigy and arms were dragged through the city of Paris to the place de Grève, in front of the City Hall, where they were strung up by the executioner and left until after the conclusion of the present peace. I saw them there several times when I was in Paris. When the effigy was spoiled by rain, the admiral's portrait was painted on a canvas, on which were written his name, family name, titles, and the reason he had been condemned, and the painting was attached with an iron chain to the aforesaid gallows. The straw effigy was taken out to the gallows of Montfaucon, outside the gates of Paris. And from the time of the aforesaid execution, all of [the admiral's] revenues were seized and turned over to the king, who took the profits and added them to the revenues from his domain.

And inasmuch as, despite the above sentence rendered against this rebel of an admiral and his execution in effigy, he did not desist in his rebellion but rather tried to completely overthrow the state of France, the king and the court of Parlement passed the following edict against him: That His Majesty would give ten thousand gold crowns to any persons, of whatever rank or quality they might be, who could apprehend or take him alive so as to turn him over to the law. Even if those who captured him were the worst criminals in the world, His Majesty would forgive their crimes, however grievous and enormous they might be. And if they could not take him alive but killed him dead, His Majesty promised to give them two thousand gold crowns, along with his forgiveness for any crimes, as stated above. This edict was published and posted on the street corners of Paris and in the king's camp.

Once the admiral knew this, he immediately hired a number of men to guard him day and night, so as to avoid being taken in this manner. They were named archers of his guard, and he had them take an oath of loyalty, just as if he were king, and he paid them very well, so as not to be betrayed by them. They served him so faithfully that anyone wanting to capture or kill him could not do so, even though more than a hundred tried, so as to have the king's forgiveness for their crimes, as well as the money he promised.

Among others who tried to execute the aforesaid order and proclamation was Monsieur de Maurevert, a Huguenot nobleman who was in the admiral's camp and one of the wickedest sorts there. [Maurevert was] an enterprising man who, once he knew of the king's proclamation and promise, sought a means to surprise the admiral so as to kill him, in part to have the money but also to regain His Majesty's favor, because he had left his service voluntarily. He did not dare do so, however, without the right opportunity. One day, he found himself in the presence of the aforesaid admiral and Lord Mouy, who were rather poorly guarded while conferring about the war. Seeing such a good opportunity and thinking to shoot the admiral, [Maurevert] instead killed Mouy, his lieutenant, and fled to the camp of the duke of Anjou, the king's brother, whom he told of his deed and asked for mercy. And the duke pardoned him and sent him to his brother [the king] to confirm his forgiveness and give him the promised two thousand gold crowns, even though he knew well that the admiral had suffered no harm. Maurevert was well received and paid the aforesaid sum by the king. He took an oath to serve the king faithfully in all his affairs and never to undertake anything against his will. In addition to giving him two thousand gold crowns, the king made him captain of a cavalry company and set him up quite well. He also gave him several men to guard him.

14

JEAN DE LA FOSSE

Reactions in Paris to the Peace
of Saint-Germain
1570–1571

The pacification edicts issued at the end of each War of Religion ordered people to forget past conflicts and live together peacefully. The Peace of Saint-Germain following the third war also explicitly ordered any monuments commemorating executions or other events connected to the wars to be torn down. One particular monument in Paris, a tall pyramid known as the Cross of Gastines, because it marked the site of a house that had been destroyed after its chief residents, Philippe and Richard de Gastines, had been convicted of heresy and executed for celebrating a Protestant Lord's Supper there, became the object of intense controversy when Parisians refused to allow the cross to be torn down. Diarist Jean de la Fosse (ca. 1526–1590), a parish priest in central Paris, recorded these impressions of the conflicts that ensued over the order to remove the Cross of Gastines. What was at issue here for Catholic Parisians? Why did they resist removing the monument so determinedly? Why were local authorities so hesitant to intervene?

August [1570]: On Friday, August 11, the peace with the Huguenots was published. They gained more from this peace than they got by the Edict of January [1562]. More specifically, they got four cities to ensure their personal security—La Rochelle, Montauban, La Charité, and Cognac—along with two locations for preaching in each province and the right of those nobles with high justice to hold assemblies and preaching in their houses. There were articles so appalling as to make France and good servants of the king tremble, especially inasmuch as the Huguenots are to be considered faithful servants of the king and all that they have done agreeable to him. There was a riot in Rouen

Jean de La Fosse, *Journal d'un curé ligueur de Paris sous les trois derniers Valois*, ed. Edouard de Barthélemy (Paris, 1866), 95, 103–6.

when the peace was proclaimed, and it is said that those who proclaimed it were injured and several killed. . . .

September [1571]: At the beginning of this month, word came again to Paris to tear down the Cross of Justice, otherwise known as the Cross of Gastines. City officials responded that they had not put it there and therefore they would not touch it. The magistrates of the Parlement said that their legal decisions were valid and they would not retract them. It was therefore ordered that the provost of Paris should take it down, but he replied that he had not handed down the decision that caused it to be erected and he had no authority over the court, and therefore those who had it placed there should be ordered to tear it down rather than him.

During this month, Gaspard de Coligny, returned to his office of admiral by the edict of pacification, was summoned by the king and came from La Rochelle to meet the king at Blois, while all of the Guise family retired from court, which meant that the king was guided in his decisions by the admiral and Marshal Montmorency.[1] . . .

November [1571]: During this time, the kingdom of France was in many ways governed by the queen mother, Catherine de Medici, Admiral Coligny, Montmorency, and others, the Guise clan being excluded, which astonished everyone, because of the infinite number of edicts handed down that were all disadvantageous to Catholics. Even foreigners were astonished, such that the Spanish ambassador, seeing everything go badly in France, returned to Spain without taking leave of the king of France.[2] . . .

The king sent an express letter to the provost of Paris,[3] written and signed in his own hand and bearing his personal seal, ordering him to tear down the Cross of Justice, otherwise called the Cross of Gastines, in these words: "You must decide whether to obey me and whether to

---

[1]François de Montmorency was governor of Paris and the Ile-de-France and a marshal in the royal army. After the Bourbons and the Guises, the Montmorencys were the most powerful aristocratic clan in France. Sons of Constable Anne de Montmorency (d. 1567), François and his three brothers were moderate Catholics and despite their religious differences remained close to their cousin Gaspard de Coligny.

[2]According to other sources, the Spanish ambassador did not leave voluntarily, but was expelled by the king for encouraging resistance to his orders.

[3]Paris had many overlapping jurisdictions. The provost of Paris (*prévôt de Paris*) was a royal official charged with overseeing police and justice in the *prévôté*, or district, of Paris. Headquartered in the old fortress known as the Châtelet, the provost of Paris and his lieutenants for civil and criminal affairs should not be confused with the provost of merchants (*prévôt des marchands*) and aldermen headquartered in the City Hall.

tear down this pyramid. I forbid you to come before me until such time as it has been torn down," and at the end . . . he threatened to remove Nantouillet, who then held the post, and put in another provost. . . .

Master Benoist[4] published a little book on the subject of the cross. The book was prohibited, the printer taken prisoner by his district constable, and copies confiscated. The court summoned Benoist and told him that he was provoking sedition, but he said no, there was nothing at all bad in what he had written.

December [1571]: On the first Sunday of Advent, Master Vigor,[5] while preaching at Notre Dame, used these words in his sermon: "that the people of Paris only wanted to prevent the removal of the Cross of Justice, otherwise known as the Cross of Gastines . . . because of their zeal for God, who endured the Cross for us, and that the people of Paris had not protested when they cut down Gaspard de Coligny, who had been hanged in effigy, which would in truth have been a service to God." . . . For what he had said, Vigor was called before the Parlement, which also summoned Monsieur de Dreux, grand vicar to the archbishop of Paris, to have him instruct the preachers to keep the people obedient. To which Vigor replied that he had in truth brought up the example of Coligny, but this was not an offense against the king's majesty because it concerned only Coligny, and as for the rest, he never intended to prompt the people to sedition but rather to encourage the obedience they owed their king, and if it really was the case that the king had ordered the cross torn down, which he could not believe, he would rather blame the king's ministers than the king for this error.

On the feast of the Immaculate Conception, December 8, people broke down the gates of the cemetery of the Holy Innocents and dumped the gates and some large stones in the hole where the Cross of Gastines was to be placed after its removal. The following day, the guards [sent to protect the cemetery] were routed by the people and forced to flee. Some fled into the church of Saint-Leu and Saint-Gilles in the rue Saint-Denis. They stashed their guns and helmets in the church vestiary and even had to disguise themselves, fearing the people, who immediately afterward went to the house of three Hugue-

---

[4]René Benoist, parish priest in Paris's church of Saint-Eustache and a prolific pamphleteer on religious subjects.

[5]Simon Vigor, parish priest in Paris's church of Saint-Paul and a celebrated preacher; archbishop of Narbonne from 1572 until his death in 1575.

nots, including one named Mercier, who lived at the sign of the Golden Hammer on the Notre Dame bridge, and smashed the windows and workshops of these Huguenots. In the crowd were a few petty pillagers, who took a few small things from the Huguenots' houses, and some were taken prisoner for this.

. . . The commander of the night watch was sent to the king to beg him not to remove the cross, on account of the riot that it might provoke. But the king sent away the commander with rigorous orders, which he also sent again to the Parlement, telling him that "that if he did not obey these orders, he would show him who was king."

3

The Saint Bartholomew's Day Massacre in Paris and the Provinces

The Attempt to Kill Admiral Coligny

15

FRANÇOIS HOTMAN

A True and Plain Report of the Furious Outrages of France

1573

After the massacre, Protestant publicists hastened to send accounts of the events in Paris to their allies in other parts of Europe. The following narrative of the wedding of Marguerite of Valois and Henry of Navarre and the initial attempt on Admiral Coligny's life comes from the first and most widely circulated of these Protestant accounts. Though published anonymously, it has been identified as the work of François Hotman, a distinguished legal scholar who barely escaped with his life when the Saint Bartholomew's Day Massacre spread to Bourges, where he taught law at the university. First published in Latin, the international language

François Hotman, *A true and plaine report of the furious outrages of Fraunce, & the horrible and shameful slaughter of Chastillion the Admirall without any respect of sorte, kinde, age, or degree*, by Ernest Varamund of Freseland [pseudonym] (At Striveling in Scotlande [i.e., London], 1573), 36–50. I have somewhat modernized spelling and punctuation but otherwise left the narrative as it appears in this original English version.

of Europe's learned elites, the work was translated into French, English, and German in 1573 so as to reach a broader audience. The following excerpt comes from the first English edition.

Like many Protestant commentators, Hotman believed that Henry, duke of Guise, who blamed Coligny for his father's death in 1563, was responsible for the initial attempt to assassinate the admiral. Responsibility for subsequent events, however, he places elsewhere.

When the day came, the marriage was with royal pomp solemnized before the great Church of Paris, and a certain form of words so framed as disagreed with the Religion of neither side was by the king's commandment pronounced by the Cardinal of Bourbon, the king of Navarre's uncle, and so the matrimony celebrated with great joy of the king and all good men, the bride was with great train and pomp led into the church to hear mass, and in the meantime the bridegroom, who disliked these ceremonies, together with Henry Prince of Condé, son of Louis, and the admiral, and other noble men of the same religion, walked without the church door, waiting for the bride's return. . . .

After the marriage ended at Paris, which was the time that the admiral had appointed to return to his own house, he moved [requested permission from] the king concerning his departure. But so great was the preparation of plays, so great was the magnificence of banquets and shows, and the king so earnestly bent to those matters, that he had no leisure, not only for weighty affairs, but also not so much as to take his natural sleep. For in the French court, dancings, maskings, stage plays (wherein the king exceedingly delights) are commonly used in the night time, and so the time that is fittest for counsel and matters of governance is, by reason of nightly riotous sitting up, of necessity consumed in sleep. So great also is the familiarity of men and the women of the queen mother's [Catherine de Medici's] train, and so great liberty of sporting, entertainment, and talking together as to foreign nations may seem incredible and be thought of all honest persons a matter not very convenient for preservation of noble young ladies' chastity. Moreover, if there come any panderer or bawd out of Italy, or any schoolmaster of shameful and filthy lust, he wins in short time marvelous favor and credit. And such a multitude is there begun to be of Italians commonly throughout all France, specially in the court, since the administration of the realm was committed to the queen mother, that many do commonly call it French-Italian, and some term it a colony, and some a common sink of Italy.

These madnesses of the court were the cause that the admiral could not have access to the king's speech, nor entrance to deal in weighty matters. But when they that were sent from the Reformed churches to complain of injuries commonly done to those of the [Protestant] religion understood of the admiral's purpose to depart, they did with all speed deliver to him their books and petitions and besought him not to depart from the court till he had dealt with the cause of the churches and delivered their petitions to the king and his council. For this cause the admiral resolved to defer his going for a while, till he might treat with the king's council concerning those requests, for the king had promised him that he would shortly attend those matters and be present with the council himself.

Besides this delay, there was another matter that stayed him. There was owing to the Reiters of Germany, which had served on the part of the Religion in the last war, great sums of money for their wages, in which matter the admiral travailed with incredible earnestness and care.[1]

Concerning all these affairs, the admiral (as he determined before) having access and opportunity for that purpose, moved [appealed to] the king's privy council the 22 day of August, which was the fifth day after the king of Navarre's marriage, and spent much time in that treaty. About noon, when he was in returning home from the council with a great company of noblemen and gentlemen, behold, a harquebusier[2] out of a window of a house near adjoining shot the admiral with two bullets of lead through both the arms. When the admiral felt himself wounded, nothing at all amazed, but with the same countenance that he was accustomed, he said, through yonder window it was done: go see who are in the house. What manner of treachery is this? Then he sent a certain gentleman of his company to the king to declare it unto him. The king at that time was playing at tennis with the duke of Guise. As soon as he heard of the admiral's hurt, he was marvelously moved, as it seemed, and threw away his racket that he played with on the ground, and taking with him his brother-in-law, the king of Navarre, he retired into his castle. . . .

---

[1]The Reiters were mercenary soldiers hired to help fight the religious wars. The king had promised to pay what was owed them but had thus far been unable to come up with the funds.

[2]A gunman firing a harquebus, a matchlock gun.

At the suit of the king of Navarre and the prince of Condé, and others, the king by and by gave commission for enquiry to be made of the matter and committed the examining thereof to three chosen persons of the Parlement of Paris, [presiding justices] de Thou and Morsan and Viole, a counselor. . . .

While these things were doing, and the admiral's wound in dressing, Teligny[3] went by commandment to the king and most humbly besought him in the name of his father-in-law that his majesty would vouchsafe to come unto him, for that his life seemed to be in peril, and that he had certain things to say greatly importing to the king's safety, which he well knew that none in his realm dared declare to his majesty. The king courteously answered that he would willingly go to him, and within a little while after he set forward. The queen mother went with him, and the duke of Anjou, the duke of Montpensier (a most affectionate subject of the Church of Rome), the count of Retz (the queen mother's great familiar [intimate associate]), Chavigny and Entragny, which afterwards were chief ringleaders in the butchery of Paris.

When the king had lovingly saluted the admiral, as he was wont to do, and had gently asked him some questions concerning his hurt and the state of his health, and the admiral had answered with such a mild and quiet countenance that all they that were present wondered at his temperance and patience, the king being much moved (as it seemed) said, "The hurt, my admiral, is done to thee, but the dishonor to me. But by the death of God," said he, "I swear I will so severely revenge both the hurt and the dishonor that it shall never be forgotten." . . .

[The king then urged Coligny to move into the Louvre, in case the Parisian populace should cause trouble, but Coligny refused.]

Therewith the duke of Anjou, the king's brother, commanded Cosseins, captain of the king's guard, to place a certain band of soldiers to guard before the admiral's gate. There could hardly a man be found more hateful against the admiral's part, nor more affected to the Guisians than this Cosseins, which the success plainly proved, as hereafter shall appear. The duke of Anjou further added that he thought it should be good for the admiral if more of his friends and familiars that lodged in the faubourgs did draw nearer about him, and forthwith he commanded the king's harbingers [quartermasters] to

---

[3]Admiral Coligny's son-in-law.

warn those to whom they had before assigned lodgings in that street to remove from hence and to place the admiral's friends in their rooms. Which counsel was such as none could possibly be devised more fit for the things that followed. For those which might have by flight escaped out of the suburbs were now held fast enough, being enclosed not only within the walls of the town but also within the compass of one narrow street. The next day after, the undermasters [district officers] of the streets, commonly called quartermen, surveyed all the victualing houses and inns from house to house, and all the names of those of the [Protestant] Religion, together with the place of every of their lodgings they put in books, and with speed delivered over the same books to those of whom they had received that commandment.

After noon, the queen mother led out the king, the duke of Anjou, Gonzaga, Tavannes, the count of Retz (called Gondi) into her gardens called Tuileries. This place, because it was somewhat far from resort [remote], she thought most fit for this their last consultation. There she showed them how those whom they had long been in wait for were now sure in hold, and the admiral lay in his bed maimed of both his arms and could not stir, the king of Navarre and prince of Condé were fast lodged in the castle, the gates were kept shut all night and watches placed, so as they were so snared that they could no way escape, and, the captains thus taken, it was not to be feared that any of the Religion would thenceforth stir any more. Now was a notable opportunity (said she) offered to dispatch the matter. For all the chief captains were fast closed up in Paris, and the rest in other towns were all unarmed and unprepared, and that there were scarcely to be found ten enemies to a thousand Catholics; that the Parisians were in armor and were able to make threescore thousand chosen fighting men, and that within the space of one hour all the enemies might be slain, and the whole name and race of those wicked men be utterly rooted out. On the other side (said she), if the king does not take the advantage of the fitness of this time, it is no doubt but that if the admiral recover his health, all France will shortly be on fire with the fourth civil war.

The queen's opinion was allowed. However, it was thought best, partly for his age and partly for the affinity's sake, that the king of Navarre's life should be saved. As for the prince of Condé, it was doubted whether it were best to spare him for his age or to put him to death for hatred of his father's name. But herein the opinion of Gonzaga took place, that he should with fear of death and torment be withdrawn from the Religion. So that counsel broke up, with appointment that the matter should be in execution the next night early afore day, and that the ordering and doing of all should be committed to the duke of Guise.

16

GIOVANNI MICHIEL

Report to the Venetian Senate on the Wounding of the Admiral

1572

Not all Protestants blamed the Guises for the failed attempt to assassinate Coligny. Some believed that Catherine de Medici was behind the attack and that she had carefully planned for the blame to fall on the Guises by arranging to have the shot fired from a house that belonged to one of their family connections. Catholic commentators were also divided on the question of who was responsible for the initial attack. One of the strongest accusations against Catherine is expressed in the report Venetian ambassador Giovanni Michiel made to the Venetian senate and doge (chief magistrate) several months after Saint Bartholomew's Day. Michiel did not personally witness most of the events in his report, but he had established a very good network of informants and, as an experienced diplomat, knew that his masters in Venice would want to know who was behind the attack and whether it was the unintended consequence of a feud between noble clans or the result of a political coup that might have a broader impact on international relations. Michiel's assessment of the situation is excerpted here.

What grounds does he offer for blaming Catherine for the attack on Coligny and the massacre that followed, and what motives does he attribute to her? Does he appear to believe that the attack was justified?

Giovanni Michiel, "The Whole Thing Was the Work of the Queen," in *Pursuit of Power: Venetian Ambassadors' Reports on Spain, Turkey, and France in the Age of Philip II, 1560–1600*, ed. and trans. James C. Davis (New York: Harper & Row, [1970]), 232–45.

The wedding and the parties and balls went on for four days without stopping, from Monday to Friday, and there were still several kinds of tournaments to be held.

Then, at the dinner hour on Friday, while the admiral was returning on foot from the court to his lodgings and reading a letter, someone fired an harquebus at him. The shot came from a window which faced a bit obliquely on the street, near the royal palace called the Louvre. But it did not strike him in the chest as intended because it so happened that the admiral was wearing a pair of slippers which made walking difficult and, wanting to take them off and hand them to a page, he had just started to turn around. So the harquebus shot tore off a finger on his left hand and then hit his right arm near the wrist and passed through it to the other side of the elbow. If he had simply walked straight ahead it would have hit him in the chest and killed him.

As you can imagine, news of the event caused great excitement, especially at court. Everyone supposed it had been done by order of the duke of Guise to avenge his family, because the window from which the shot was fired belonged to his mother's house, which had purposely been left empty after she had gone to stay in another. When the news was reported to the king, who happened to be playing tennis with the duke of Guise, they say he turned white and looked thunderstruck. Without saying a word he withdrew into his chambers and made it obvious that he was extremely angry.

Great numbers of Huguenots and the admiral's friends and followers were in Paris at this time for the marriages of Condé and the king of Navarre. . . . They all hurried directly to the admiral's lodgings and even though it was not yet known whether the shot was fatal or whether he would lose the arm, they yelled and threatened that that arm of the admiral would cost more than forty thousand other arms. Some of their leaders went to where the king was dining and complained violently and bitterly. They demanded swift and stern justice and said that otherwise there was no lack of men who would provide it. Among them was a certain Captain Briquemault, who was later dragged out of the English ambassador's house, where he had hidden, and was jailed and ultimately hanged. According to what Briquemault revealed, the Huguenots assembled that same day bearing arms and came very close to carrying out a plan to march on the Louvre (where the king lives and also the duke of Guise), overpower the royal guards and any others who blocked their way, and kill the duke in his apartment. If it had come to this there would have been great danger of an all-out battle in which most of the nobility would have been killed, because there were a great many of them in both factions. In their fury the Huguenots might not have spared even the king's brothers or the king himself. But Briquemault persuaded them not to do it, or so he claimed.

To return to the admiral, after dinner the same day the king, the queen [mother], and Monseigneur [the duke of Anjou] paid a visit and urged him to move to the palace, where he would be safer and more easily looked after. The king told him that he had had some of the duchess of Lorraine's rooms prepared for him. But he thanked His Majesty and said he was quite comfortable where he was. They say that after the king left the admiral told those who were with him about this offer of rooms in the palace and said, "Only a fool would let them lead him between those four walls!" But as we shall see, as long as he was in any building in the city he was already in the king's power.

All of the above happened on Friday. On Saturday the admiral's dressings were changed and the word was given out—which may or may not have been true—that the wound was not a mortal one and that there was no danger even that he would lose the arm. The Huguenots only blustered all the more, and everyone waited to see what would happen next. The duke of Guise knew he might be attacked, so he armed himself and stuck close to his uncle, the duke of Aumale, and as many relatives, friends, and servants as possible.

But before long the situation changed. Late Saturday night, just before the dawn of Saint Bartholomew's Day, the massacre or slaughter was carried out. The French say the king ordered it. How wild and terrifying it was in Paris (which has a larger population than any other city in Europe), no one can imagine. Nor can one imagine the rage and frenzy of those who slaughtered and sacked, as the king ordered the people to do. Nor what a marvel, not to say a miracle, it was that the common people did not take advantage of this freedom to loot and plunder from Catholics as well as Huguenots, and ravenously take whatever they could get their hands on, especially since the city is incredibly wealthy. No one would ever imagine that a people could be armed and egged on by their ruler, yet not get out of control once they were worked up. But it was not God's will that things should reach such a pass.

The slaughter went on past Sunday for two or three more days, despite the fact that edicts were issued against it and the duke of Nevers was sent riding through the city along with the king's natural brother to order them to stop the killing. The massacre showed how powerfully religion can affect men's minds. On every street one could see the barbarous sight of men cold-bloodedly outraging others of their own people, and not just men who had never done them any harm but in most cases people they knew to be their neighbors and even their relatives. They had no feeling, no mercy on anyone, even those who kneeled before them and humbly begged for their lives. If one man hated another because of some argument or lawsuit all he had to say was "This man is a Huguenot" and he was immediately killed. (That happened to many Catholics.) If their victims threw themselves in the river as a last resort and tried to swim to safety, as many did, they chased them in boats and then drowned them. There was a great deal of looting and pillaging, and they say the goods taken amounted to [were worth] two million because many Huguenots, including some of the richest of them, had come to live in Paris after the most recent edict of pacification. Some estimate the number who were killed as high as four thousand, while others put it as low as two thousand.

The killing spread to all the provinces and most of the major cities and was just as frenzied there, if not more so. They attacked anyone, even the gentry, and as a result all the leaders who did not escape have been killed or thrown in prison. It is true that Montgomery[1] and some others who were pursued by the duke of Guise escaped to England, but they are not major figures. And the king has terrified them enough so they won't make any trouble.

In birth and rank the chief [Huguenot] leaders are Condé and the king of Navarre, but they are boys who have no followers. What's more, they are in the king's power and might as well be in prison. It will be a long time before they will be allowed away from the court, and they will be lucky if they are not treated worse than they are now, especially Condé. I must not forget to tell Your Serenity that after the wounding and the murder of the admiral someone told the king that Condé was going around and making threats, so the king had him brought to him and said, "I hear you are making threats. All right! I'll have you put on the block and tell the executioner to chop off what little you have in the way of a head!" So then Condé bowed humbly and begged for mercy. This Condé is a young fellow sixteen or seventeen years old, with a face which looks proud, but also scowling and

[1]Gabriel de Lorges, count of Montgomery, was the captain of the Scottish Guard who mortally wounded King Henry II in a tournament in 1559. Although he killed the king by accident, Catherine de Medici never forgave him and pursued him as much on that account as because he was a Huguenot leader. He was captured and killed in 1574.

gloomy; we would say he has a "threatening brow." And his manners are as bad as his looks, the result of growing up during the rioting and civil wars. He looked on the admiral as an idol and a father. But there is no danger now that he or any others will raise the banner again. The Huguenots, reduced in number to two thousand, have taken up arms so as not to be slaughtered and they have gathered in their old refuge of Sancerre on the Loire River. But it won't be hard for the king to besiege them and starve them out. . . .

At present, sermons, meetings, and all other activities of the new sect are forbidden. Both nobles and commoners are returning to the Church, especially since the leading families are showing them the way. The prince of Condé and his wife have publicly abjured, and so has Mme. de Crussol (a great friend of the queen) and many other ladies. The king of Navarre has recanted and ordered that Catholicism be reestablished in his lands, monasteries set up again, and the churches allowed to have their revenues. And that's not all. The Huguenot ministers themselves, including the most important ones, want to become Catholics again! But with these men they will handle the abjurations more carefully than they did with the others.

There were two kinds of Huguenots in France. One group was made up of rebels and atheists who used religion only as a pretext and encouraged the growth of the sect because it led to wars in which they profited from the plundering and the looting and the good pay they got as soldiers and officers. These men would fight against anyone, even the king. The other kind had flocked to the new sect only because they wanted to enjoy more freedom and license, but they kept out of the riots and rebellions and obeyed the king. There is nothing to fear now from the first group because the leaders and others who could disturb the peace are all dead or being killed. The second group may not change their real beliefs but they have no choice but to continue to obey the king if they want to enjoy the presents and favors and titles he distributes. The king is an absolute ruler and just as he can shower rewards on those he likes, so he can ruin and make life miserable for those he despises and chooses to forget. The French are so constituted that they cannot and will not live anyplace but in France; they would never dream of it. They have no God but the king, and the common people fall on their knees and worship him when he passes by, just as if he were God. So we can state this as a general proposition: everywhere, but especially in France, whatever religious beliefs the king holds, his subjects must do the same.

Serene Prince, there are different opinions as to whether the death of the admiral and what was done to the Huguenots was spontaneous or planned. I think I should tell Your Serenity what I have managed to learn from some very important people who are in on the secrets of the government. I can state to Your Serenity that from start to finish the whole thing was the work of the queen. She conceived it, plotted it, and put it into execution, with no help from anyone but her son the duke of Anjou. She first had the idea a long time ago, as she recently reminded her cousin, Monsignor Salviati, who is the nuncio[2] there. She told him not to forget and to bear witness (as he does) concerning a message she sent to him secretly to carry to the late pope. The message was to the effect that he and the king would soon see themselves avenged on the Huguenots.

This was the reason, moreover, why the queen worked so hard to arrange her daughter's marriage to the king of Navarre and passed up important marriage offers from Portugal and other quarters. She wanted to have the marriage take place in Paris, calculated that the admiral and the other important leaders on that side would attend, and that there was no better way to get them there. . . .

As for the harquebus shot, which I said was thought to have been the work of the duke of Guise,[3] he knew nothing about it. He would never have dared to do such a thing against the king's will, because His Majesty would have taken offence, and while he might have concealed his anger for the time being he could later have done Guise and his family grave harm by keeping the duke out of his service and his favor. But as things now stand others have amply carried out Guise's vengeance for him without his giving any thought to it, and his standing and favor at the court rise higher with each passing day. He is an attractive person who is very popular with the king and everyone else, and his ardor and bravery on the battlefield have shown him to be a worthy son of his father.

They say, therefore, that the attempt with the harquebus was plotted by the duke of Anjou and the queen. And they also say, but in a whisper (and it would be best if we kept it to ourselves), that there was no Frenchman they trusted for the job, so they had it done by a Florentine officer named Piero Paolo Tosinghi. Everyone who has lived

[2]The pope's representative.

[3]In the initial dispatch that another Venetian envoy, Michele Suriano, sent the doge on August 25, 1572, he reported that the Huguenots all blamed Henry, duke of Guise, for the initial attempt to assassinate Coligny.

in France knows about Tosinghi, who has an outstanding reputation as a soldier, and it is known that a few days after the shooting he boasted about it to one of his cronies. The official story, however, is that it was done by a Frenchman named Maurevel [Maurevert], a professional marksman who once killed a famous Huguenot officer named Mouy with an harquebus shot. But nothing was seen of him and he never turned up as one would have expected.

After the harquebus shot on Friday they had to arrange the rest of the business, so the queen and the duke of Anjou closeted themselves in the royal study with the king—just the three of them were there— and told him how matters stood. The queen showed him that the rebels were virtually caged within the walls of Paris, so that he had a perfect opportunity to get his revenge on them safely and easily. She pointed out that he could make up for the shame he had incurred by making peace with them and that since he had only done that out of fear and compulsion he was not obliged to live up to the treaty. Then she made him see how deceitful and treacherous the admiral had been in advising him to make war, when this would have meant ruin for a kingdom which was already exhausted and debt-ridden. She also pictured the disgust other rulers would have for him if he went to war without the slightest justification against a king with whom he had such a close family tie.[4] And she made him consider the most important point of all, that if the admiral survived, the civil war would surely resume because he and his followers would be determined to have their revenge. In short, they had to forestall him before it was too late.

With these and some other well-grounded arguments it was easy for the queen to convince the king she was right. Her task was helped by the fact that on that same day a Huguenot leader named Bouchavannes (now dead) had come to them secretly and revealed a secret Huguenot battle order. They were to assemble with all their infantry and cavalry on September 5 at Melun, which is thirty miles from Paris, and then attack the unsuspecting king and have their revenge for the injury to the admiral. So [Bouchavannes had said] they had better make careful preparations. This is the conspiracy which the king later told the Parlement had been discovered against the queen, his brothers, and himself, and he added his brother-in-law and the king of Navarre [to the list of intended victims] to make the plot even more shameful.

---

[4]Philip II of Spain had married Charles's sister Elizabeth in 1559. She died in 1568 but left a daughter.

As soon as the king had been won over by his brother and the queen, they called in the provost of the merchants, an able man named Marcel[5] whom they knew they could rely on. They asked this Marcel how many Parisians the king could count on to help him in a time of need, and he answered that it would depend on how much time there was to get them together. "Suppose there was a month," they said; "then you could have 100,000," he told them, "or more than that if the king needed them." "If there was a week?" they asked. "A proportionately smaller number," he said. "And what if there was only one day?" "At least 20,000," he told them. They swore him to absolute secrecy and commanded him to give the same oath to the chiefs of the parishes and tell them that that same night they must order one man in each household to stay on the ready with arms and a torch. This command was carried out so carefully and secretly that no one even knew what his neighbor was doing; and precisely because no one knew the reason for the orders everyone stayed alert to see what would happen.

After they dismissed Marcel they called in the duke of Guise and gave him and his uncle (the duke of Aumale) and the king's natural brother the assignment of murdering the admiral, his son-in-law Teligny, and any followers who were with him. They told Marshal Tavannes and the duke of Nevers, both of them trusted men and great enemies of the Huguenots, to do the same to the count of Rochefoucauld (despite the fact that he was a favorite of the king) and some other important men. (I mention these details because I imagine Your Serenity will be happy to hear them.) You can imagine how delighted the duke of Guise was to be given this task, and how enthusiastically he carried it out. Since I wrote dispatches to you about this I won't go into details about the death of the admiral—how [Guise's men] found him, and stabbed him, and, thinking he was dead, threw him out the window as the duke and the others insisted so that they could see him. The first to strike him was a German who used to be a page for the late duke of Guise, and when the admiral saw him coming near he said, "Young soldier, have pity on an old man!" I will also leave out the details about how after his murder the common people savagely defiled and abused the corpse, and how his head, hands, and genitals were cut off and he

---

[5]The merchants' provost was the equivalent of mayor. In fact, city elections held just a week earlier had replaced Claude Marcel with Jean Le Charron. Marcel was well-known at court, however, and had a long record of Catholic activism, so he may have accompanied Le Charron to the meeting.

was hung by his feet at the public scaffold outside Paris called Mont-faucon. You have read about all these things.

All the leaders and important men I have mentioned who lived near the court were killed at daybreak, and the ordinary people knew virtu-ally nothing about it. But then they heard the news, and the king gave the order that all the other Huguenots in Paris should also be mur-dered and robbed, and things began to happen with all the fury I have described. However, many nobles and other prominent people who could pay money or promised to pay it later were rescued and hidden in the king's brothers' residences with their consent, and even in the lodgings of the duke of Guise himself. The same happened to a lot of others who were in good standing or were friends or relatives of the king's men. As for [Huguenot] noblewomen, their houses were sacked but great care was taken to spare their lives, and none of them were killed. As a matter of fact, the queen sent coaches to bring them to court and sheltered them there. The king wanted to know who were being protected and commanded that everybody report them or pay severe penalties. When he heard that two of his officers had taken a payment of twenty thousand francs to shelter a man named Cavaignes (the chief secretary of the admiral, later hanged), he ordered them to bring him the man immediately. In the presence of a crowd of people he told them, "If you don't bring him you'll pay with your own heads." So they brought him! Those who were reported were taken out of their hiding places and put in several prisons, as if they were in stor-age, and every night they took ten or so to the river and drowned them. And that's not all. Army officers and others were sent into the countryside to kill some of the better-known Huguenots who hap-pened to be in their houses there and plunder their belongings. It makes one think of Sulla and his proscriptions.[6]

This procedure added to the general terror, even though the king went to the Parlement after the massacre in Paris and promised that he would respect the recent edict of pacification, stop the looting and killing, and obey the country's laws and customs by prosecuting the guilty with the customary forms of trial and punishment. This was not done, however, nor is it being done now, and this is why all the Huguenots who have the means have gone to live outside France until the frenzy subsides and they can see how things will turn out. The

---

[6]Sulla was a Roman general and dictator (138–78 B.C.E.) famous for his pitiless methods, which included proscription—outlawing by fiat a potential enemy, who could then be summarily executed and his estates added to the treasury.

fact is that the Catholics are just as angry as the Huguenots, not so much about the fact of the massacre, they say, as about the way it was done. That a man can be alive in the evening and dead the next morning seems to them something foreign and they say this way of doing things—using naked power and ignoring the forms of justice— amounts to tyranny. They blame this on the queen, saying that she is an Italian from Florence, and a Medici at that, and therefore she has tyrant's blood in her veins.

The Killing Widens

17

CLAUDE HATON

The Catholic Response to a Huguenot Plot
1572

Like many Catholic accounts of Saint Bartholomew's Day, Claude Haton's narrative is framed in terms of a Huguenot plot. In this excerpt, he begins by stating that the king and Catholic princes had been warned of a Huguenot plot to forcibly massacre them.

And so they resolved to do to the Huguenots what the Huguenots wanted to do to the king and princes, and as soon as possible, so as to act before the date they had chosen. The Huguenots' strength and armed might was the motive for this royal resolution, inasmuch as it was not possible to employ legal proceedings, because the Huguenots all had their arms at the ready. It was entirely certain that if the king had proceeded through ordinary legal channels, he would not have succeeded, and he and the princes of the blood and other Catholics

Claude Haton, *Mémoires contenant le récit des événements accomplis de 1553 à 1582*, ed. Félix Bourquelot (Paris, 1857), vol. 2: 672–76.

would have been in grave danger. There was no doubt about this. And so, having duly considered this all, His Majesty decided to take the course of action to save the noble blood of France.

After the king, the Catholic princes of the blood, and the Guises had resolved to forestall the Huguenots and to do the same thing to them that the Huguenots planned to do to their majesties and highnesses, they had to figure out how to dexterously execute their plan so that they would benefit from it, as would the Catholics of Paris and other parts of the Most Christian Kingdom. They agreed that the enterprise could not be well executed without the help of the captains and governing officers of Paris, and that it was therefore necessary to make use of their persons and means. All of the Catholics in Paris had their arms ready in their houses to protect themselves against a Huguenot attack and to defend their lives and properties against them, because of their arrogance and the threats they had uttered ever since the attempt to assassinate the admiral. If they tried to attack the Huguenots without first warning the Parisians, the Parisians, rushing out in arms, would throw themselves against their fellow Catholics, believing them to be the Huguenots who wanted to attack them. This would cause such disorder, with Catholics and Parisians killing one another, that it would give the Huguenots the chance to do just what they had plotted against the king, the princes, and the city.

Catholic Parisians were advised very secretly of the wishes of the king and princes, which occasioned great joy. They then agreed together on the means for accomplishing the affair and the best day and time. Because it was necessary to anticipate the Huguenots and the day they had decided on for massacring the king, princes, and Catholics, everything had to be agreed upon quite quickly. The day decided on was August 24, after 11:00 P.M., the evening of the feast of Saint Bartholomew. The bell in the clock tower of the Palais de Justice would serve as the signal to take up arms and rush out into the streets and attack the houses where Huguenots were lodged, including both residents of the city and visitors.

The first Huguenots who were seized by the Catholics were the admiral, the king of Navarre, the prince of Condé, and La Rochefoucauld, the principal leaders of the plot against the king and the Catholic princes and their households. The king of Navarre and prince of Condé were spared, and no harm was done to them, but none of their men were pardoned. Instead, they were massacred in Navarre and Condé's presence and under their very feet. The admiral was massacred in his room, along with all who were present, and his body thrown out the window onto the pavement below. The prince de la Rochefoucauld and all his men were left there. The noise made by the attack on the households of the Huguenot princes and admiral caused the Paris night watch to take up arms and go out into the street and the bell in the clock tower of the Palais de Justice to be rung. Catholic Parisians put a certain insignia on their clothes similar to that worn by the king's men, so as to recognize one another in the melee.

18

Report by the Merchants' Provost
August 23, 1572

Municipal records affirm that the city was called to mobilize late on the night of August 23 on the grounds that the Huguenots were conspiring against the crown. According to city records, the merchants' provost (the equivalent of a mayor) communicated the following orders to the other city officers, who carried them out as well as possible beginning Saturday night. How might these orders have contributed to the subsequent violence?

Today, Saturday, August 23, 1572, President Le Charron, the merchants' provost, was summoned by the king to his castle of the Louvre very late in the evening. His Majesty told the merchants' provost in the presence of the queen, his mother, and of milord the duke of Anjou, his brother, and other princes and lords, that he had been warned that those of the new religion were conspiring to rise up against His Majesty and against his state, and to disturb the peace of his subjects and of the city of Paris. His Majesty explained this at greater length and gave the merchants' provost more details, and told him how some great nobles and rebels of the aforesaid new religion had conspired against him and his state this very night and had even sent him haughty and menacing threats. For these reasons, he wanted

François Bonnardot, *Registre des délibérations du Bureau de la Ville de Paris* (Paris, 1893), 7:10–11.

the merchants' provost to make arrangements and give orders for the security of the queen mother, his brothers, and his kingdom, and for the peace and tranquillity of the city and of his subjects.

And in order to ward off the aforesaid conspiracies and prevent the execution of their evil plots, he enjoined and commanded the merchants' provost to seize the keys to all of the gates of the city and to carefully lock them, so that no one could enter or leave the city, and to bring all of the boats in the river over to the right bank, to chain them up, and to be sure that no one was able to use them to cross the river. Also to arm all of the captains, lieutenants, ensigns, and bourgeois of the quarters and districts of the city capable of bearing arms, and have them at the ready in the districts and major intersections of the city, so as to receive and execute His Majesty's orders, as he found fit and necessary.

His Majesty also commanded the aforesaid merchants' provost and aldermen of the city to diligently oversee the execution of these orders and also to hold the city's artillery ready both within the City Hall and in front of it on the place de Grève, both to defend and protect the aforesaid City Hall and to use elsewhere as necessary.

His Majesty commanded these things along with several other orders, which he gave to the merchants' provost in particular and to him, the aldermen, and the city collectively.

19

FRANÇOIS DUBOIS

Painting of the Saint Bartholomew's Day Massacre in Paris

This etching reproduces the earliest known painting of the massacre. The artist, François Dubois, died in Geneva in 1584 and may have been a survivor of the massacre. The actions depicted here would nevertheless seem to have been drawn from Protestant histories and not from personal observation. The artist imagines Paris from the vantage point of a viewer standing near the bank of the Seine and looking west toward the

Bibliothèque nationale de France.

100

palace of the Louvre (left of center in the background) and the house where Coligny was killed (center right). The church of Saint-Germain des Prés stands on the opposite bank of the river, with the gate through which the Huguenots lodged near Saint-Germain fled depicted in the background. What is the artist trying to tell us about both victims and perpetrators through the details in the image?

Victims and Survivors

20

SIMON GOULART

Memoirs of the State of France under Charles IX

1578

Simon Goulart (1543–1628), a Protestant minister nearly caught up in the massacre, published a collection of pamphlets and narratives concerning Saint Bartholomew's Day under the title Memoirs of the State of France under Charles IX *in 1577. Continuing to collect new information on both the victims and their killers from Huguenot refugees arriving in Geneva, he republished the work in expanded editions in 1578 and 1579 and later incorporated these narratives into four enlarged editions of* The Book of Martyrs *begun by the Genevan printer Jean Crespin. The passages excerpted here recount the death of a prominent magistrate and then, more briefly, the murders of some of the more prosperous Protestant merchants and their families.*

Although we can confirm from archival sources that the individuals named here did indeed die in the massacre, there is no way to verify the accuracy of the specific details Goulart collected from refugees. Even Catholic sources recount enough atrocities, however, to force us to conclude that the sorts of violence depicted here did indeed occur. With some

[Simon Goulart], *Mémoires de l'estat de France sous Charles IX*, 2nd ed. ([Geneva], 1578), fols. 295, 300–303.

caution, then, we can use these narratives to gain insights into the psychology and behavior of those who participated in the popular killings. How can we reconcile motives such as personal gain and revenge with the religious hatreds let loose in the massacre? And why do women and even infants appear to have been killed in particularly gruesome ways?

The narrative also offers good insights into the moral principles of its Protestant author. How does Goulart memorialize Pierre de La Place as a Christian martyr? What values is he trying to instill in his readers?

Sunday was employed in such killing, raping, and pillaging that it is believed that the number killed on that day and the two that followed in Paris and its suburbs is more than ten thousand persons, among them great lords, gentlemen, presiding magistrates and judges, artisans, women, girls, and boys. The streets were covered with dead bodies, the river tinted with blood, and the doors and gates to the king's palace painted with the same color; but the killers were not yet sated.[1]

The commissioners, militia captains, *quarteniers*,[2] and district officers all went with their men from house to house, wherever they thought they might find Huguenots, breaking down the doors, then cruelly massacring those they encountered, without regard to sex or age, having been incited to do this by the dukes of Aumale, Guise, and Nevers, who went through the streets calling out, "Kill, kill them all; the king commands it." Carts piled high with the dead bodies of noble ladies, women, girls, men, and boys were brought down and emptied into the river, which was covered with dead bodies and red with blood, which also ran in various other places in the city, such as the courtyard of the Louvre and surrounding areas.

. . .

We shall begin with Monsieur Pierre de La Place, a presiding magistrate in the Cour des Aides,[3] and recount in more detail what happened to him, as he well deserves on account of his virtue.

---

[1] Goulart borrowed this paragraph from the *Wake-Up Call for the French and Their Neighbors* (Document 22).

[2] Paris was divided into sixteen quarters, each of which was subdivided into smaller districts for purposes of local administration. A *quartenier* headed each quarter.

[3] A sovereign court charged with adjudicating disputes over taxation.

Sunday, about six in the morning, a man named Captain Michel, one of the king's harquebusiers, came to La Place's house, where he gained entry all the more easily because he was believed to be one of the king's Scottish Guards. . . . Having gained entry, this Captain Michel, armed with a harquebus on his shoulder and a pistol in his belt and wearing a white handkerchief around his left arm as a sign that he was one of the killers, first announced that the duke of Guise had by the king's orders killed the admiral and several other Huguenot lords, and that inasmuch as the rest of the Huguenots, whatever their social status, were destined to be killed, he had come to Monsieur de La Place's home to exempt him from this calamity, but that he wanted them to show him all the gold and silver in the house. Upon hearing this, La Place, astonished at the presumptuousness of this man, who, though alone in the house amidst ten or twelve people, dared to use such language, asked him where he thought he was and whether there was not a king. At this, the captain, cursing, responded that he should come along then and speak to the king, and that he would hear what the king's will was. Hearing this, and suspecting that there was some great uprising in the city, La Place slipped out the back door of his house, hoping to seek shelter with some neighbor. Meanwhile, most of his servants vanished, and the captain, having already received about a thousand gold crowns before he departed, was asked by La Place's daughter, Lady des Maretz, to take her and her husband, Sir des Maretz, to the home of a Catholic friend, which he agreed to do. Then La Place, having been refused shelter in three different houses, was forced to return to his own, where he found his wife extremely upset and tormented by fear that the captain would throw her son-in-law and daughter in the river, as well as by the terrible danger in which she found both her husband and all her household. But Sir de La Place, fortified by the spirit of God with an unbelievable steadfastness, chastened her rather severely, reminding her how such afflictions should be received meekly and as coming from the hand of God, and, after speaking a bit about the promises God makes to his own, he reassured her.

Then he ordered that the servants who remained in the house be called, and once they had assembled in his chamber, as they were accustomed to doing each Sunday for the exhortation he customarily made to his family, he began to pray. He next read a chapter from the book of Job, along with John Calvin's exposition or sermon on the subject, and, having discoursed on the justice and mercy of God, whom, he said, like a good father tests his elect by various chastisements, so that they do not become focused on the things of this world, he reminded them how necessary afflictions are to the Christian and that it is not in the power of either Satan or the world to harm or injure us, except to the extent that God willingly permits it. One must nevertheless not fear their power, which extends only to our bodies. Then he began again to pray to God, preparing both himself and all of his family to endure all sorts of torments, even death, rather than to do anything contrary to God's honor.

When his prayer was finished, they came to tell him that Sir de Senesçay, the king's provost, and several of his archers were at the door, demanding in the king's name that he admit them and saying that he had come to save La Place and prevent the house from being pillaged by the populace. Hearing this, La Place ordered the door opened to him. When Senesçay had entered, he told them about the great slaughter of Huguenots throughout the city by the king's command. . . . Nevertheless, he had the king's express order to prevent any harm from coming to La Place but was instead to bring him to the Louvre, because the king wanted to be instructed by him in several matters concerning the affairs of those of the new religion, for which he [La Place] had some responsibility, and thus he should prepare to come before His Majesty. Sir de La Place responded that he would be very happy to have the opportunity before leaving this world to render an account to His Majesty of all of his actions and activities, but given the horrible massacres being committed throughout the city, it would be impossible for him to get as far as the Louvre without grave and certain danger to his person. It was [Senesçay's] responsibility to ensure his safe passage to the king, leaving in his house as many archers as he thought best until the popular fury had calmed. Senesçay agreed to this and left one of his lieutenants named Toutevoye, along with four archers, in the house.

A short time after Senesçay's departure, presiding magistrate Charron,[4] then serving as the merchants' provost of Paris, arrived at the house and, after speaking privately with him [La Place] for some time, left again, leaving behind four of the city's archers alongside Senesçay's. All the rest of the day and the following night were spent blocking and walling up the entrances to the house with strong logs and piling rocks and paving stones on the windowsills, so that, by their careful and diligent guard, it appeared that these archers had been put inside

---

[4]Jean Le Charron was also a presiding magistrate in the Cour des Aides and thus a colleague of La Place.

the house to exempt La Place and all of his family from the common calamity, until Senesçay, returning the next day at two in the afternoon, announced that he had the king's express commandment to bring [La Place] to him, and he must no longer put this off. Monsieur de La Place protested, as before, the dangers that awaited in the city; that very morning a nearby house had been pillaged. Senesçay nevertheless insisted, saying that the Huguenots always claimed that they were the king's humble and obedient subjects, but when it was time to obey His Majesty's orders, their ardor cooled and they backed away in horror. As for the danger in going to the Louvre, Senesçay responded that he would give him one of the Paris captains who was well known to the people to accompany him. As Senesçay was saying this, Captain Pezou, one of the principal troublemakers, entered La Place's chamber and offered to accompany him. La Place instantly refused, telling Senesçay that this was one of the cruelest and most wicked men in the city, and he begged him, if he could postpone going to the king no longer, to personally accompany him, to which Senesçay replied that, because he had other things to take care of, he could not accompany him more than fifty paces.

On hearing this, La Place's wife, because of her great love for her husband and despite being a woman on whom God had bestowed his grace and benedictions, threw herself at Senesçay's feet and begged him to accompany her husband. But La Place, who showed no sign of losing courage, moved to raise his wife up again, correcting her and telling her that we must not look to men to protect us but rather to God alone. Turning, he saw on the hat of his eldest son a paper cross that he had put there in a moment of weakness, thinking to save himself by this means,[5] and scolded him sharply, ordering him to remove that sign of rebellion and reminding him that the true cross we had to bear was the tribulations and afflictions that God sent us as an indisputable sign of the happiness and eternal life he prepares for his own. Then, seeing himself strongly pressured by Senesçay to proceed to His Majesty and reconciled to the death that he saw being prepared for him, he took up his coat, kissed his wife, reminding her above all else to keep the honor and fear of God always before her, and went out with a light heart. In the rue de la Verrerie, across from the rue du Coq, certain murderers awaited him with daggers bared. At about 3:00 P.M., they killed him like a poor sheep, still surrounded by the ten

---

[5]In addition to a white armband, the Catholics had adopted a white cross as an insignia by which they might recognize one another during the riots.

or twelve of Senesçay's archers who accompanied him. His house was thoroughly pillaged during the five or six days that followed. His soul having been received in heaven, Monsieur de La Place's body was carried to a stable at the City Hall, where his face was covered with dung. The next morning, it was thrown in the river.

. . .

Mathurin Lussault, jeweler to the queen mother, living in the rue Saint-Germain, near the sign of the Mirror, hearing the bell at his window ring, went downstairs and as he opened the door was run through by the gold-drawer[6] with a thrust of his sword. Lussault's son, hearing the noise, came downstairs immediately and was struck hard in the back by a sword. In spite of this, he escaped to a tailor's house, but the latter refused to let him in, and so he was finished off by a vagrant, who, searching him, found in his trouser pocket a beautiful clock worth seven or eight hundred gold crowns. When he saw this, the gold-drawer began to berate the vagrant and was ready to kill him, saying that he was poaching on another's territory. But the other having defied him, the gold-drawer went to report this all to the duke of Anjou, who gave the murderer ten crowns for the clock. The household's servant, a girl of sixteen, escaped into the house of a velvet weaver who insisted that she promise to go to Mass. When she refused, the murderers came along and killed her.

After having thus killed Lussault, they closed the door and left. His wife, Françoise Baillet, an honorable woman, having heard from a young lad named René what had happened to her husband and son, climbed to the attic and, opening a window to escape into the courtyard of her neighbor, as others had previously done, fell so hard that she broke both legs. The murderers, returning to find the window open and the house empty, so threatened the neighbor (who had hid her in his cellar) that he betrayed her. Then they took her and dragged her by the hair some great distance through the streets and seeing that she had gold bracelets on her arms but lacking the patience to unfasten them, cut off both wrists. And as she deplored their extreme cruelty, a meat roaster who was in the group ran a

---

[6]A gold-drawer was an artisan who drew out gold wire into the fine threads used for ornamental trim and embroidery. The gold-drawer referred to here is also mentioned in other narratives of the massacre as one of the most active killers.

skewer through her body, where it remained lodged. Several hours later, her mutilated body was dragged into the river. Her hands lay for several days on the pavement and were gnawed at by dogs.

A very rich jeweler named Monlouet, asleep alongside his wife, did not hear the pounding at his door. She was not asleep and promptly got up and opened it. The murderers raced up the stairs and, without giving a moment's reprieve to this honorable person, killed him in his bed. His wife, who was very pregnant, gathered a child of eighteen months into her arms and tearfully begged for his life, or at least that they take pity on the infant still within her womb. But instead of being moved to compassion, these tigers bristling with rage tore the child that she held from her arms and cast him to one side on the ground. Then they came at the poor woman and ran her through with a sword, such that during the next several hours one could see the baby she was carrying breathe and then die. Two women from Rouen who had taken up lodging in the house several days earlier were also killed and the entire house pillaged.

Philippe Le Doux, a notable merchant jeweler, having recently returned from the fair at Guibray, was in his bed. His wife had the midwife with her because she was ready to give birth. Hearing some-one demand entry in the name of the king, although she was unwell, she went and opened the door to the murderers, who killed her husband in his bed. The midwife, seeing that they wanted also to massacre the pregnant woman, begged them insistently to wait until she had delivered the child, who was the twenty-first that God had given her. After having wrangled about this for a bit, they took this poor creature, already half-dead of fright, and plunged a knife up to its hilt into her anus. Feeling herself mortally wounded but nevertheless desiring to bring forth her fruit, she fled into an attic, where they pursued her and gave another dagger blow to her belly, then threw her out the window giving onto the street. The infant pushed its head out of her body and yawned, to the great astonishment and confusion of some Catholics, who were forced to recount it a number of times, while detesting the cruelty of the executioners. The embroiderer, a companion of the gold-drawer, was the principal murderer.

Pierre Feret, a silk cloth merchant living in the rue Saint-Denis, near the sign of the Good Shepherd, was still in bed when his wife's nephews came banging on his door demanding that it be opened in the name of the king. Having entered, they said to him, "Uncle, today you and our aunt, who have been so stubbornly opinionated, are going to the devil." And without respect for kinship or any apology whatsoever, they took them to the Poupin horse trough, quite some distance away. The wife, who remained resolute and calm in appearance, gave her silver belt to a washerwoman she knew as she left the house and encouraged her husband as they went along. Once they had reached their destination, they were clubbed to death; their own nephews had a hand in it, and their bodies were thrown in the water.

21

CHARLOTTE D'ARBALESTE

Escape from the Massacre

1572

In August 1572, Charlotte d'Arbaleste was just twenty-two years old and a widow. Her first husband, Jean de Pas, seigneur (lord) of Feuquères, had been killed in the third War of Religion. She had come to Paris to settle some business affairs when the Saint Bartholomew's Day Massacre broke out. In fact, she had been planning to leave Paris the next day to stay with a sister in the countryside but was instead overtaken by the events. Arbaleste's account of her perilous escape from the city, excerpted here, illustrates well the explosion of popular hatred that produced the massacre but also the contradictory elements of mercenary greed and human decency that allowed some Huguenots to be saved. At the same time, it shows the complexity of the religious situation and the competing loyalties of families divided along religious lines.

Because I intended to leave on the Monday after Saint Bartholomew's Day, I planned to go to the Louvre on Sunday to take leave of the princess of Conti, the duchess of Bouillon, the marquise of Rothelin,

Charlotte d'Arbaleste, *Mémoires de Madame de Mornay*, ed. Madame de Witt (Paris, 1868), 59–63. The date given here is that of the events the document describes. Arbaleste gave a preliminary copy of the memoirs to her son in 1595, but the date when she began to compose them has never been established.

and Lady Dampierre. But when I was still in bed, one of my kitchen servants, a Protestant and native Parisian, came to find me and, very frightened, told me that they were killing everyone. I was not immediately worried but, having put on my petticoat, looked out the window and saw in the rue Saint-Antoine where I was lodged an agitated populace and several platoons of troops, each wearing a white cross on his hat. Then I realized that it was true and sent word to my mother's, where my brothers were staying, to find out what was happening. There they were all astir, because my brothers professed the true religion [Protestantism]. My maternal uncle, Pierre Chevalier, the bishop of Senlis, sent word to gather up my most important things, saying that he would send someone for me very soon. But as he was preparing to send for me, he received word that his brother, Charles Chevalier, the lord of Esprunes, who was an ardent Protestant, had been killed in the rue de Bétisy, where he had lodged so as to be close to the admiral [Coligny]. This caused Monsieur de Senlis to forget me, besides which, when he went out into the street, he was stopped and only escaped with his life because he agreed to cross himself, which he did willingly, as he had no understanding of the true religion. Having waited half an hour for him, and seeing the popular disturbances increasing in the rue Saint-Antoine, I sent my daughter, who was then three and a half, in the arms of a servant to the home of Monsieur de Perreuse, who was a master of requests in the king's household[1] and one of my dearest relations. He brought her in through a back door and sent word that if I wanted to come too, I would be welcome. I accepted his offer and found myself the seventh to do so. He did not at that point know all that had happened, but having sent one of his servants to the Louvre, he learned of the death of the admiral and so many lords and noblemen and also that the violence had spread across all of the city. It was then 8:00 A.M. I had barely left my lodgings when servants of the duke of Guise arrived there and asked for me. They looked everywhere for me and, not finding me, sent word to my mother that if I would bring them one hundred gold crowns, they would save my life and valuables. My mother sent word of this to Monsieur de Perreuse's, but after having thought about it, I decided that it was not a good idea to let them know where I was or to go to them. Instead, I begged my mother to tell them that she had no idea what had become of me but, at the same time, to offer them the

---

[1] A magistrate with special responsibility for cases brought before the king's council but also considered a part of the Parlement.

money they demanded. When they did not find me, my lodgings were pillaged.

[Meanwhile, Monsieur de Perreuse took in more than forty people.] So as to avoid suspicion, he was forced to send to the other end of town for supplies. He also stationed himself or his wife at the door of his house, so they could say a few words in passing to Monsieur de Guise, Monsieur de Nevers, and the other lords who came by the house repeatedly, and the same with the militia captains who were pillaging neighboring houses. We were there until Tuesday, but no matter how good a face he put on things, he could not avoid suspicion, so that orders came for his house to be searched on Tuesday afternoon. Most of those who had taken shelter there left to go elsewhere; only Mademoiselle de Chaufreau and I remained. We had to be hidden, she with a servant in a woodshed behind the house, one of my servants and me in a hollow roof vault. The rest of our servants disguised and hid themselves as best they could. From this hollow vault, high in the attic, I heard such strange cries of men, women, and children being killed in the streets below that I was unable to think clearly and almost in despair. Had I not feared offending God, I almost would have preferred to jump to my death than to fall alive into the hands of the populace or to see my daughter, whom I had left below, killed, which I feared more than my own death. One of my servants took her and crossed through all of these dangers to find Lady Marie Guillard, dame d'Esprunes, my maternal grandmother, and left her there, where she remained until my grandmother's death. On this Tuesday afternoon, President de la Place of happy memory was killed in the very street where Monsieur de Perreuse stood, in the rue Vieille du Temple, while they pretended to be taking him to the king. In order to protect us and save his house from being pillaged, Monsieur de Perreuse, seeing himself so threatened and in danger from all sides, sought help from Monsieur de Thou, the king's attorney general and currently a presiding magistrate in Parlement.

Having escaped this fury more easily than expected, it was nevertheless time for us to disguise ourselves and move on. I could not go to my mother's, because they had placed guards in her house, so I went to the house of a blacksmith who had married one of her chambermaids. He was a violent man and captain of his district, but I told myself that he would not harm me because of the benefits he had received from her. My mother came to see me there that night; she was more dead than alive and more paralyzed with fear than I was. I spent that night with the blacksmith militia captain, and I heard nothing but the Huguenots being vilified and saw the plunder of their pillaged houses being brought in. He told me in the strongest terms to go to Mass.

[The following day, Arbaleste's mother sought shelter for her in the house of another presiding magistrate in the Parlement, but this too became dangerous because the family had Protestant relatives who were being sought there. So late on the night of Thursday, August 28, the family had her taken to the home of a grain merchant who was one of their trusted retainers. She stayed there five nights. During this time, her mother, who had convinced Arbaleste's brothers to save their lives by going to Mass, tried without success to convince her to save herself in the same way. Eleven days after the massacre began, she took passage on a boat on the Seine to escape the city, where she was still in danger. Her trials were not yet over. She finally reached the safety of Sedan, an independent principality on France's northeastern border, more than two months after her flight began.]

The Role of the King

22

The Wake-Up Call for the French and Their Neighbors

1574

Although Charles IX was generally believed innocent of plotting to lure the Protestant aristocracy to Paris with the specific intent of murdering them in their beds, some Protestant publicists nevertheless accused him of participating actively in the killings once he had agreed to their necessity. The following account of Charles's role in the attempt to assassinate Huguenot nobles lodged in the faubourg of Saint-Germain, across the

---

Le reveille-matin des françois, et de leurs voisins. Composé par Eusebe Philadelphe Cosmopolite, en forme de Dialogues (Edinburgh, 1574), 1:61–63. Authorship of the treatise is disputed. Robert Kingdon surmises that it was a collaborative effort and published in Strasbourg rather than Edinburgh. See Kingdon, *Myths about the St. Bartholomew's Day Massacres, 1572–1576* (Cambridge, Mass.: Harvard University Press, 1988), 70–71.

river from the Louvre, comes from The Wake-Up Call for the French and Their Neighbors, *one of the earliest and most successful propaganda pieces published in the wake of the massacre. It first appeared under a different title in Latin and French editions early in 1573. The French edition bore a Basel imprint but was in fact published in the Huguenot stronghold of La Rochelle, which became the focus of the fourth War of Religion when its Protestant leaders refused allegiance to the crown in protest against the massacre. It was republished in an expanded form along with a second dialogue in 1574 (Document 32) in the hope of gaining support for the Huguenots' rebellion both within France and abroad. Parts of its narrative also were borrowed by Simon Goulart and other Protestant writers and turn up later in the* Memoirs of the State of France *(Document 20) and other works, giving them an even wider audience.*

Fortunately, the lord of Fontenay, Monsieur de Rohan's brother, the vidame[1] of Chartres, the count of Montgomery, the lord of Caumont, one of the Pardillans, Beauvais la Nocle, and several other Huguenot lords and gentlemen were lodged in the faubourg of Saint-Germain, across the river from the Louvre. And God willed that Marcel, the merchants' provost of Paris, although he had been commanded by the king on Saturday evening to hold a thousand armed men ready at midnight to assist Maugiron (to whom he had given orders to take care of those in the faubourg, as well as commanding the commissioner of the district and controller du Mas to guide him and his troops to the Huguenots' lodgings), did not have his men ready, and the commissioner du Mas slept past the assigned hour. In addition, a certain man (who has not been seen or heard from since), having seen what had been happening all night to the Huguenots in the city, took a little dinghy across to the faubourg of Saint-Germain and warned the count of Montgomery at about five o'clock on Sunday morning of what he knew. The count of Montgomery sent word to the vidame of Chartres and other Huguenot lords and gentlemen lodged in the faubourg. Several of them, unable to persuade themselves that the king was I won't say the author but simply consenting to the killings, resolved to cross the river in boats to go and find the king, much preferring to trust in him than, in fleeing, to show they were suspicious. Others were suspi-

---

[1]A noble title similar to "viscount" or "count."

cious but, believing the plot was against the king's own person, wanted to be near him so as to humbly serve him and, if necessary, die at his feet. But a very short time later, they saw in the river, coming straight at them, two hundred or so armed members of the king's guard, crying "Kill, kill," and shooting their harquebuses in the sight of the king, who was in the window of his room. This was about seven o'clock on Sunday morning. I have also been told that the king, taking a hunting harquebus into his hands and denying God, said, "Let us shoot; let us shoot. For God's sake, they are fleeing." At the sight of this spectacle, the Huguenots from the faubourg did not know what to believe and were obliged to flee—some on foot, some on horseback; some with their boots on, some without—leaving all that was most precious to them, in order to save their lives, to wherever they thought they would have the safest refuge. They had not yet all left when the king's soldiers and Swiss Guard, along with some courtiers, sacked their lodgings, killing all those whom they found still there. . . .

The entire day of Sunday, August 24, was spent killing, raping, and pillaging, such that the number killed on that day in Paris and the faubourgs is believed to be more than ten thousand persons, including lords, gentlemen, presiding magistrates and counselors [in the sovereign courts], lawyers, students, doctors, solicitors, merchants, artisans, women, girls, youths, and preachers. The streets were covered with dead bodies; the river tinted with blood; the doors and entrances to the king's palace painted the same color. But the killers were not yet sated.

The king, the queen his mother, his brothers, and their ladies went out in the evening to see all the dead. Among others, the queen mother wanted to see Lord Soubise, to learn if it was true that he was incapable of relations with his wife.[2]

About five in the afternoon on Sunday, criers announced to the sound of trumpets that everyone was to return to their homes and those already in their houses were to stay there. Only soldiers of the guard and the Paris commissioners with their troops were to go about the city in arms, with serious penalties for those who disobeyed.

Many who heard the announcement thought the affair was winding down, but the next day and those following, it began again.

---

[2]Catherine's alleged curiosity had its origins in rumors that Soubise's wife was seeking to terminate her marriage on grounds of his impotence. Whether or not Catherine did go out to look at Soubise's dead body, this story caught the imagination of Protestant memoirists and is reproduced in Dubois's painting of the massacre (Document 19).

23

CHARLES IX

Declaration on the Reasons
for the Admiral's Death

August 28, 1572

The contradictory statements that Charles IX issued in the wake of the massacre do more to obscure than to clarify his role in these events. On August 24, he sent letters to the governors of a number of French provinces explaining that violence had broken out as a result of the old quarrel between the admiral and the Guises. The Guises, he said, knew that the admiral's friends blamed them for the attempted assassination and decided to ward off the vengeance they anticipated by attacking first. Expressing regret that he had been unable to prevent the violence stemming from these clan rivalries, he explained that his guards had had all they could do just to keep him and his brothers safe in the Louvre. "Nothing in this," Charles added, "is to nullify the edict of pacification, which, to the contrary, I want observed as strictly as before," and he concluded with orders to keep the peace and prevent similar uprisings elsewhere in the country.[1] Within a few days, however, Charles had changed his tone. Instead of blaming the Guises and their quarrel with Coligny, he blamed the Huguenots and said that it had been necessary to act quickly to ward off the conspiracy they had formed against the crown. Copies of the following letter were sent to provincial governors on August 28. A number of Protestant commentators have claimed that the letter was accompanied by oral orders or by another letter saying to kill any Protestants found outside their homes, but no such letter has been found and the charge has never been proved. Why might Charles IX have changed his position and decided to claim responsibility for ordering the Huguenot leaders killed?

---

[1]"Lettre du Roy au gouverneur de Bourgogne," as reproduced in *Archives curieuses de l'histoire de la France*, ed. Louis Lafaist (pseud. L. Cimber) and Félix Danjou, 1st series (Paris, 1835), 7: 133–35.

"Déclaration du Roy de la cause et occasion de la mort de l'admiral et autres ses adhérants et complices," as reproduced in *Archives curieuses de l'histoire de la France*, ed. Louis Lafaist (pseud. L. Cimber) and Félix Danjou, 1st series (Paris, 1835), 7:162–64.

His Majesty desiring to make known to all his lords, gentlemen, and other subjects the cause and occasion of the death of the admiral and his adherents and accomplices that occurred recently in this city of Paris on August 24, insofar as the event may have been portrayed to them other than it actually was,

His Majesty declares that all that occurred was by his express commandment and not for any religious reasons nor in contravention of his edicts of pacification, which he as always intended and still wishes and intends to observe, keep, and undertake, but rather to ward off and prevent the execution of an unfortunate and detestable conspiracy by the admiral, its head and author, and his adherents and accomplices against the person of the king and his state, the queen his mother, his brothers, the king of Navarre, and other princes and lords close to them.

For which reason His Majesty wishes to make known by this present declaration and ordinance to all gentlemen and others of the pretended reformed religion that he wishes and intends that they may, in all security and freedom, live and reside with their wives, children, and families in their homes under the king's protection, just as they have previously done and may continue to do in accordance with the terms of the edicts of pacification.

Commanding and ordering very expressly to all governors and lieutenants general in each of his regions and provinces and to all other of his magistrates and officers to whom it pertains not to attempt, permit, or allow [actions] of any sort to be undertaken against the persons and properties of members of the aforesaid religion, their wives, children, and households, on penalty of death.

Nevertheless, to avoid any troubles, scandals, suspicion, or mistrust that might occur because of preaching and assemblies that might take place either in the houses of the aforesaid gentlemen or elsewhere, as is permitted in the edicts of pacification, His Majesty very expressly prohibits and forbids all of the aforesaid gentlemen and others of the aforesaid religion to assemble for any reason until the king, after having provided for the tranquillity of his kingdom, orders otherwise, on penalty of imprisonment and confiscation of property.

And also very expressly forbidding, on the same penalties, all those who for the above-mentioned reasons have taken or retained prisoners to demand any ransom from them and to immediately inform the provincial governors and lieutenants general of the name and legal state of the aforesaid prisoners, whom His Majesty orders released and freed, unless they are the leaders who have command over those of the [Protestant] religion or who have undertaken actions or schemes on their behalf and might have knowledge about the aforesaid conspiracy, in which case they are to immediately inform His Majesty, so that he can tell them what he wishes done.

Ordering also that in the future no one shall be so bold as to take and hold prisoners for the above-mentioned reasons without the express commandment of the king or his officers, nor shall they chase down and take from fields, farms, and estates any horses, mares, bulls, cows, or other livestock; property, fruits, grains, or anything whatsoever; nor interfere with or harm farmers but rather let them do their work in peace and security, on the above-mentioned penalties.

Issued in Paris on the 28th of August 1572.

Signed CHARLES
Beneath: Fizes

The Killing Spreads to the Provinces

24

JOHANN-WILHELM VON BOTZHEIM

The Massacre in Orléans
1573

With a population of 45,000 to 50,000, the Loire Valley town of Orléans was the fifth-largest city in France in the mid-sixteenth century. Like other towns that responded to news of the massacre in Paris with killings of their own, Orléans had a significant Protestant population and a history of troubled relations between this group and the Catholic majority. The fact that it had been seized by the prince of Condé's Huguenot army in one

---

"Le massacre fait à Orléans au mois d'août 1572, duquel fut témoin, et faillit lui-même être victime, Joh.-Wilh. Von Botzheim, auteur de la relation qu'on va lire," *Bulletin de la Société de l'histoire du Protestantisme français* 21 (1872): 345–92.

of the opening moves of the first War of Religion had left a legacy of hard
feelings and distrust, even after the city returned to Catholic control.
Orléans was the home of an important law school with an inter-
national student body. One of the German students caught up in the mas-
sacre, Johann-Wilhelm von Botzheim, left a vivid eyewitness account of
how news from Paris touched off a wave of religious violence in Orléans.
The narrative suggests that, as in Paris, fear of a Protestant coup
prompted a militant reaction on the part of the city's Catholics. Clearly,
the memory of Condé's seizure of the city in 1562 remained strong. It is
interesting, moreover, that the city's provost was initially suspicious of the
order to kill the Protestants and did not believe that the king would have
commanded such a thing. But can we trust Botzheim's assertion that
captains sent to verify the order confirmed it, or was he merely persuaded
of this by the same hearsay and rumors that prompted the citizens of
Orléans to round up and kill their Protestant neighbors?

I have reported on all that I could gather while in Paris about the massacre in that city according to information gathered from the most
trustworthy men. I now come to the infernal butchery in Orléans,
which I will depict from a closer perspective and, so to speak, from
real life, as I was present there myself.

The news arrived in Orléans that the admiral had been wounded by
a harquebus shot. The Huguenots received this news the twelfth Sunday after Trinity, which fell on August 24, while they were returning
from services. As the message said that the king was very agitated
and wanted to avenge the crime, they took the news rather calmly.
That evening, a messenger arrived who demanded immediately to see
the city's provost, Monsieur L'Arinier,[1] to whom he delivered a packet
of letters bearing the royal seal. These letters contained the account of
what had happened to the admiral and other Huguenots of Paris and,
in addition, the order to do the same to all the Huguenots and to
exterminate them, taking care not to let the order leak out so as to
take them by surprise. As the provost was a prudent and circumspect
man, these instructions appeared to him implausible, especially inasmuch as he had been sent by the king to Orléans to pacify any uprisings that the turbulent population of the city might attempt and, in
ensuring everyone's rights, to bring about a return to law and order,

---

[1]This name is probably wrong; the provost was Monsieur de la Renie, a president of
the Parlement of Dijon, who had been sent to Orléans to deal with earlier disorders.

which no longer existed on account of the perversity of the judges. He had also been given the mission of making sure the Huguenots were not molested. And while he could not ignore the disfavor with which the king regarded those of the Reformed religion, . . . he could not comprehend such orders, especially at the very moment when the marriage of the king's sister was to be an occasion for eternal peace with the Huguenots. He also recalled what had just been learned about the admiral's injury and the king's intentions to see justice done. Given these reflections and others of the same sort, the provost, while not wanting to reveal anything to the Huguenots, considered these messages suspect. Thinking that they might have been forged by the Guises so as to incite some tumult, he ordered the messenger held in prison and at the same time had two captains given horses and sent off at a full gallop to find out the truth.

The captains traveled night and day, thereby returning on Monday, and they confirmed the news received previously. They also made things worse and aggravated the situation by telling the provost all about the massacres, which were still going on. The provost, meanwhile, even before their return, had stationed papists at the city's gates and on its ramparts. This was done at 5:00 A.M. on Monday, so that if the worst came to pass, the papists would have the drop on the Huguenots and not the other way around, as had occurred in previous troubles. As soon as the news of this measure spread among the papists, six hundred archers gathered on Monday morning before one of the city's gates with the intention not just of making themselves masters of the city but also of exterminating the Huguenots at the same time. This the provost employed all of his energies to prevent, and having been warned in time, he constrained them just to guard the gates. In brief, this guarding of the gates did not bode well and meant that the Huguenots were caught unawares. Every day the rumors grew, and the confirmation of the news from Paris inflamed the people more and more.

Obrecht[2] warned me as of dawn that the city was occupied. This was something new for me, something I had never seen. Looking out from the house, I could see the papists milling about in arms. The mistress of my lodgings, my landlady, who was Catholic, told me not to be afraid, that everything would be all right and that the papists would restore order. They would not be caught off guard today as they had been too often before. In the meantime, my brother went

---

[2]One of the other German students in Orléans.

with Monsieur Barbin to see if all of the gates were occupied by men in arms. He found that they were and also the street corners. One of the captains warned him not to leave his lodgings. It was not, he said, the time for a stroll. If any of the Huguenots went outside, they were quickly despoiled of their clothing and hats. One could feel from moment to moment the outbreak of violence approaching. . . .

All of the street corners were provided with sentinels and the guard of the city as a whole entrusted to ten captains, each of whom had command over a designated group of soldiers. . . .

The Huguenots hid wherever and however they could, since they had been taken by surprise and knew the cruelty of the people of Orléans. Everything bad was happening all at once; it was necessary to save one's property but also one's life. On all sides the papists began not just to pillage but also to kill. The preceding days, they had mostly given themselves over to pillaging and extortion. They first extorted from their victims all they could by way of money while promising to save their lives; then, when they had taken everything else, they took their lives as well.

During the days that followed, the massacres did not diminish in the center of town; they [the "papists"] especially searched in the places known to be frequented by Huguenots. In particular, they sought those known as the elders of the church, and I know that several had their throats cut most despicably. The orders said first to get rid of all of the leaders among the Reformed, after which they could more easily take care of the rest. Desiring to follow the Parisian example, they especially sought out the city councilors, notables, lawyers, and all the men distinguished by either their authority or their intelligence. The Huguenots hastened to turn over a part of their valuables to Catholics with whom they had previously had ties of friendship or intimacy. Many people brought us objects that could be hidden in the trunks that were confided to the care of our landlady and of Madame Floccard and Madame de la Chaise, our neighbors. Others threw their valuables into their latrines or wells; still others buried their most precious belongings or hid them in their walls or other secret places. . . .

We learned shortly thereafter that a German had been killed and that Birckheimer, Botzen (?), and Mecken had had their properties pillaged.[3] We asked our landlady to go alone (since the rioting prevented us from going with her) to see the provost, Monsieur L'Arinier, to tell

---

[3] Other German students in Orléans; one name was apparently unclear in the record.

him who we were, explain our condition, and ask for his protection for her house. She managed to get in to see him, even though he was very tied up by the popular fury, and received a rather lukewarm response; that is to say, he admired her for daring to bring him such a request, given that she was not safe herself in her house, and he advised her nevertheless to keep us shut up in our lodgings, for we were not the ones the king intended to do away with. The man found himself in a difficult position, for he did not want the Huguenots to be treated with such cruelty and barbarity, but the demands and relentlessness of the captains and people forced him to submit to their will. The captains wanted him to have it announced to the sound of trumpets throughout the city that any and all papists were to strangle all of the Huguenots without exception. When he refused to give this order, they threatened (just at the moment that our landlady was intervening on our behalf) to cut off his head. His resistance made him odious in the eyes of the people, and because of his opposition, some took him for a Huguenot. In order to avoid the people's rage, he was forced to take refuge in the citadel, the highest stronghold in the city, and to surround himself with a personal guard. He did not come out until Marshal Cossé[4] arrived in Orléans and even then never left his side when going about the city.

With law and order thus suspended for three whole days, the people gave full vent to their rage and each enjoyed full liberty to pillage at his pleasure and to rob, murder, and butcher the Huguenots. A great number of cruelties, barbarities, and acts of savagery were committed during this time. People talked about nothing except the massacres, extortions, and thievery of all sorts. More than four hundred peasants and farmers came into the city so as to pillage and steal, in recompense for the losses they had suffered during previous troubles. They butchered and massacred the unfortunate Huguenots without mercy. . . .

On Sunday, all the churches were filled with people. Thousands of widows and orphans, youths and little children who customarily went to Protestant services went to hear Mass. They presented themselves en masse for Communion. All of these unfortunates were obliged to abjure; they had to sign a formula of abjuration. These abjurations were a real torture for them. Monsieur Favre told me about them. The widowed women among our neighbors—Mesdames de la Chaise,

---

[4]Artus de Cossé-Brissac was the king's lieutenant governor for the region.

Coursière, and Grison—all went through with this; I had hoped they would prefer to risk their lives for their religion. When Obrecht counseled Madame Coursière, who customarily detested and execrated the Mass and did not hesitate to say so, not to do anything against her conscience, she broke into tears and fell back on the weakness and frailty of her sex. The rumor was that women who did not renounce their beliefs would be put to death and that they had killed not more than forty during the troubles in Orléans. They also rebaptized children who were six, seven, or eight years old but let them live. The king's orders were to kill all of the children over twelve or thirteen....
That same Sunday, all the papists were happy and gay; they feasted all day and shared out the spoils of their victims. And when the time came that the Huguenots usually went out to their services and sentinels placed themselves at the gates to protect them, the "papists" chanted, "Where are the Huguenots? O, the poor Huguenots, they go to services now but there are no guards to protect them! By God's blood, let them go to the devil," and similar things....

The number of dead is uncertain. Some say as many as two thousand. If that is too high and a lower estimate is called for, it must nevertheless be at least fifteen hundred. Given the size of the city, and by comparison with the number who died in the far larger city of Paris, this figure of fifteen hundred is not a small thing.

25

The Massacre at Troyes

1572

Troyes, the seventh-largest city in the kingdom with a population of roughly thirty thousand, lay southeast of Paris in Champagne and remained an important trading center on the route from Italy and Lyons to the Low Countries. Normally at least a three-day ride from Paris, Troyes received news of the massacre by the evening of August 26, a sign

"La Saint-Barthélemy à Troyes," Bibliothèque nationale de France, Ms. Dupuy 333, fols. 65v–75r. The manuscript is undated but appears to have been written soon after the events it describes.

of the news bearer's haste. The following anonymously authored account of subsequent events in Troyes offers interesting points of comparison with accounts of events in Paris and Orléans. Here, too, the evidence concerning the king's responsibility for the massacre is open to interpretation, as are the respective roles played in the violence by local officials, members of the local militia, and unnamed hooligans or thugs.

When news of the massacres and horrible killings in Paris and lists of the principal noble victims arrived in Troyes, guards were set at the gates and all those of the [Protestant] religion who tried to leave the city were put in prison.

Monsieur de Ruffe, or Rouphe, traveling in great haste, spoke with the guards at the Croncels gate and asked them how things were going in the city. When the guards replied that things were rather peaceful, he said, "What? Don't you know what has been done in Paris and that the king intends this to be done everywhere? You can be sure that the king will not be happy with you and you will regret your disobedience to him. As for me, I am governor of a small territory and am going there in haste to execute his will. You will hear about this, for I will spare neither great nor small."

Then the bishop of Troyes, Monsieur de Bauffremont, having no patience to wait for further information or orders, met together with those of the same mind as himself, and they decided to assemble all of the town's *mauvais garçons* [hooligans or thugs] in order to kill all the Huguenots in one night. When this was decided, they were all notified and assembled at nine o'clock in the cloister of the church of Saint-Pierre, in the house of a man named La Galie. . . .

When everyone had assembled there, however, the decision was changed, and most returned home, except for some who were already accustomed to entering at night into houses that seemed easy to pillage. When the town's merchants learned about this from someone who was in danger on this account, they formed a troop of sixty or eighty horses to go through the city between about two and three in the morning and nine and ten at night. But the hooligans, knowing that the patrol would pass, made sure to stay in someone's house until it had passed and then immediately went about their plans, taking all they could carry. . . .

People had begun to attack and kill those of the [Protestant] religion who ventured out into the street during daytime. This got worse, and they broke into houses to pillage and kill. . . . I do not know the number, but here are the names of those whom I knew: Jean Rousselet, Etienne Marguin, Claude La Gueulle, Pierre Blancpignon. The latter, a pewterer, was well hidden in his house, where a pile of straw in his attic concealed a locked door and, behind it, a passageway leading to his neighbor's attic. The house was well secured, and people could not get in no matter how they tried. Then the provost's men arrived and demanded to enter by the king's authority and, having entered, seized Blancpignon and took him outside. As he was preparing to go out, he saw the armed thugs who awaited him, and among them Jean Despine, his mortal enemy, inasmuch as he had previously had Despine arrested for theft, with the result that he had been whipped through the streets of the city.[1] Seeing this, Pierre Blancpignon walked out with his hands clasped together and his eyes raised to heaven. He had not gone four or five steps when they began to strike him. Jean Hasse ran a sword through his body; Jean de Compienne, a stocking maker, struck him twice with a dagger. Thus, with blows from swords, daggers, knives, and stones, he was killed and slaughtered and then stripped naked and dragged into the river near the Comporté gate, where there is more garbage and filth than water.

The magistrate, learning what had been done, came with his guards to Blancpignon's house, which was being pillaged, and made both those who pillaged and those who just watched go away.

Jean Robert was also killed; so was Auber Margerre. Nicolas Le Brodeur's wife, seeing such disorder, said, "You reenact [Christ's] Passion, but God will exact vengeance." She was immediately seized and stabbed with knives and daggers and thrown in the river from the bridge of the Hôtel-Dieu-le-Comte. Then they hauled her out, took off her clothes and shoes, and let the current take her.

While these things were taking place, the magistrate sent for one called Captain Villiers. . . . He was charged by the magistrate with assembling a company to go out through the little towns and villages where they thought there might be members of the [Protestant] religion to seize them night or day. The company scoured the countryside up to fifteen leagues outside of Troyes and even seized papists, who escaped with some difficulty after paying a ransom.

As soon as the greatest massacres were accomplished in Paris, Monsieur de Guise sent his company hastily toward Lorraine to guard

---

[1]Rather than serving jail terms, people convicted of theft often received such corporal punishments.

all the roads and passages to Germany and Switzerland. By this means, they killed many Huguenots who had thought to escape.

Pierre Belin [who had been sent to Paris to protest against the permission recently given to Protestants to worship at a site near the city] returned from Paris to Troyes with letters from the governor of Champagne, Monsieur de Guise, which concluded with the statement that they were to believe entirely what Belin told them and to do what he said, which, as declared in the city council chambers in the presence of the magistrate, Monsieur de Saint-Falle [Anne de Vaudrey, seigneur de Saint-Phal], and the mayor and aldermen, was that they were to immediately execute all those of the [Protestant] religion and rebels against the king, as had been done in Paris. A number of members of the council were astonished at this cruel order. Those who did not want to consent to it withdrew, then the magistrate and the five or six most seditious members of the group determined to carry out Belin's instructions.

On September 3, at the hour of vespers, Monsieur de Saint-Falle charged Sergeant Pernet to go to the prisons with the soldiers who were guarding the Huguenot prisoners and slit their throats. Hearing this, Pernet took fright, remembering the reproaches he had endured during the peace concerning those who had been killed by him and others in these same prisons during the first troubles. He went home, where, sad and pensive, he went to bed without supper, as he says. The next day, he presented himself very early at the magistrate's home, where the magistrate said to him, "Well, Pernet, has it been done?" "No, Monsieur," he replied, "because I was ill last night." At this, the magistrate grabbed his dagger angrily. Seeing this, Pernet said, "As you wish, Monsieur," to which he [the magistrate] replied that it must not remain undone. That morning, after having given the prisoners breakfast, the guards were told that the judges were coming to the prisons and the prisoners must all be locked up together, which was done. Then Pernet, having with him all of the soldiers who guarded the prisoners, had Maître Jean Le Jeune, a solicitor, summoned and handed him a piece of paper. Le Jeune began to read it and then threw himself to his knees, crying for mercy and raising his hands to heaven, and begging Pernet to have pity on human blood. "Here is the pity I have for you," Pernet replied, striking him with a halberd,[2] such that he was the first killed. They killed all the others in a similar fashion, summoning them one by one and giving them

---

[2]A common weapon consisting of a battle-ax on a six-foot pike.

several blows before cutting their throats. These are the names I have been able to gather of the dead:

[A list of thirty-six names follows. A number are identified as merchants and others as artisans but none as gentlemen or elites.]

Two of the dead were not Protestants; one was in prison for debt and the other for theft.

26

CONSULS OF LIMOGES

Extract from City Registers
1572

The capital of the remote and largely rural Limousin in France's central highlands, Limoges was one of the cities that did not experience a massacre. The fact that the town had only a small Protestant population may have been one reason for this; the response on the part of local officials was another. How did the actions taken by the consuls of Limoges upon hearing news of the massacre in Paris differ from the reactions of governing authorities in Orléans and Troyes?

The harvest had been rather good in the Limousin in this year of 1572, by comparison both with previous years and with the scarcity prevailing in neighboring regions. People were living in peace and beginning to relax a bit and recover. Everyone hoped thus to pass the rest of the year, and already the consuls were proposing to offer themselves a little repose and freedom from worry, inasmuch as they considered the peace better established through the marriage of the king of Navarre and Madame Marguerite solemnized in Paris at the beginning of the month of August, after the death of the queen of Navarre in Paris the previous June.

J. Bonhoure, "Le Protestantisme à Limoges, 1572," *Bulletin de la Société de l'histoire du Protestantisme français* 20 (1871): 427–31.

The next to the last day of August, the head steward of Lord Decosse, a friend of the city, passing through this city in haste, spoke privately to one of the consuls and told him that Friday, August 22, the admiral had been wounded by a harquebus shot by a soldier lying in ambush for him. The bullet had pierced his arm and shattered a finger. All of that day and the next, members of his faction, using threats and promises of vengeance, had pressured the king to set this right. This had prompted the discovery of the detestable conspiracy on the part of the admiral and his followers against His Majesty, his family, and all of the great lords of his court, which had in turn prompted after midnight the beginning of a great and bloody massacre in which the admiral had been killed in his lodgings, thrown from a window into the street, and his abandoned body covered in mud by the people of Paris to shame and spite him. The count de La Rochefoucauld, the Pardilhans, Captain Pilles, and a great number of other noted lords and gentlemen belonging to this party had been struck down at the same time. The consul, having heard this discourse in private, begged [the messenger], on account of the importance of the affair, to come to the City Hall, where, in the presence of most of the consuls and a number of the prominent residents of the city, who had hastily assembled, he recounted in detail the truth of the tragedy, which he had witnessed firsthand. This first and more-than-strange news of so sudden and unforeseen a change was so far from the thoughts and opinions of these men that it seemed more like a distant dream than a true and actual story. Nevertheless, the importance of the affair, the danger that could follow, and the desire the consuls and all good citizens had to preserve the state of repose and security the city enjoyed awoke them from their reverie and easily persuaded them that the entire narrative was true but also that each in his heart wished to see them [the city's residents] entirely delivered from the old injuries, miseries, and torments of the past troubles.

It was thus first discussed how to ensure the city's security and to prevent a surprise attack on the part of internal or external enemies, if such there might be. To this end, eight district officers were chosen to take arms and organize the city's residents into eight groups under their leadership and direction. It was also resolved to hire thirty soldiers attached to Gabriel Raymond, the city's captain, to guard the most dangerous parts of the city walls. Overall direction, responsibility, and command was reserved entirely to the consuls, who would delegate to the district officers and their men responsibility for guarding the gates and walls as they saw fit for the safeguard and defense of the city. Thus they began from this very day to set watch and guard both day and night. Three days later, a parcel arrived from the king confirming this news and commanding them to keep everything secure and calm. A few days later, news spread that the admiral's body had been dragged through the city of Paris and then hung by the feet with its head cut off at Montfaucon; that everyone belonging to the new religion at Orléans—some twelve hundred or more—had been massacred; and, in addition, that the same had happened to all of those in Lyons and several other cities in the kingdom. From one day to the next, for a month, one heard no other news; eventually word came that those of the [Protestant] religion in Bordeaux had received the same treatment as the others. All of these examples served as arguments for the residents of this town who wanted to do the same to the inhabitants who professed this religion, who were few in number.

The consuls, fearing disturbances, called together the most notable inhabitants from all social groups and ranks for several meetings, during which it was resolved of a common accord that one magistrate and one consul, aided by two district officers and their troops, would make the rounds of the various guardhouses at night, in military order, in order to prevent any break-ins and acts of violence. The decision was based on two principal considerations: first that the king's officers and consuls had not received any orders to act as other cities whose governors had received such orders had; but also that if the people began freely to take up arms, it was to be feared that they would use them imprudently as they wished and not only against those of the [new] religion, but rather against the principal residents who were rumored to have well-stocked houses or stores. However, it was agreed to write to the king to learn his wishes, so that His Majesty should know that the inhabitants were agreed upon entirely following his private and public will. These decisions were executed in a diligent and well-ordered way, and in order to resolve the matter as quickly as possible, a man was sent to court for this purpose. By these means, they held off the massacre that some had planned and organized and nearly begun in the city.

4

Repercussions of the Massacre in France and Abroad

Reactions

27

NICOLAS PITHOU

Huguenot Conversions in the Wake of the Massacre

The Saint Bartholomew's Day Massacre had a devastating impact on the Protestant population in France. A large number of those lucky enough to escape with their lives took the path of exile and moved to Geneva or other places where they could practice their faith in peace. Many more, unable or unwilling to leave their homes, submitted to the strong pressure that was placed on them to convert and formally reconciled themselves with the Catholic Church. The following passage from the manuscript history of the Reformed church of Troyes left by pastor Nicolas Pithou (1524–1594) describes the impact of the killings on Protestant survivors in that city.

Nicolas Pithou, "Histoire ecclesiastique de l'eglise de la ville de Troyes," Bibliothèque nationale de France, Ms. Dupuy 698, fols. 392v–394r. There is no way to know exactly when Pithou composed this part of his history, but his detailed account of the massacre was clearly based on evidence collected immediately after these events.

But above and beyond all of these pitiful things that were then to be seen, the saddest and most lamentable was that most of those who had previously professed the Protestant religion and taken Communion in the Lord's Church lost no time in returning to the Mass—some out of fear, others (so dazed were they) without being forced. In short, this was a horrible occurrence, and one that no one had ever thought could happen, that out of so many people who had shared in the Lord's Supper and openly professed the Protestant faith, there remained in the city only twenty who retained their purity and did not pollute themselves with the abominations of the papacy. . . .

About six days after the massacre, the clerics elected a penitentiary priest to hear the confessions of Protestants who wished to return to the bosom of the Roman Catholic Church. The one called to this charge is named Nicolas Henry, a priest and chaplain of the chapel of the Savior, in the church of Saint-Pierre in Troyes. All those returning to the Roman church were required to present themselves before him in this chapel, bareheaded and on their knees, to confess into his ear, detest their past actions, abjure the Protestant faith, and ask his pardon and absolution. After they did all that, the priest absolved the excommunication that they had (so he said) encountered by law on account of the crime of heresy, then he gave them a written note certifying that they had fulfilled the obligation of presenting themselves, which was to serve as a letter of good standing. This done, they were to go (as some who went through this wicked process later reported) and present this certificate to the magistrate, who recorded it in a register, which they then had to sign. After that, they were given letters of protection and security, so that in the future they would not (as they were told) be bothered or pursued. The penitentiary priest had regular days and hours to receive the confessions and abjurations of those who recatholicized, and he received six pennies per head. And if some who were still capable of a bit of shame wanted to come on a special day and time, so as not to be seen by so many people, they could do so in paying each ten sous.[1] In brief, this venerable penitentiary made lots of profit in just a little time from a wicked and false commodity. For, horrible and lamentable as it was to see, they flocked to him in troops, as if to a remedy or protection, but one that was in truth

---

[1]There were twelve pennies (deniers) to the sou. The penitentiary thus made twenty times as much from each Protestant who made a private abjuration as from those who abjured publicly.

mortal for all those who, having received it, were lulled to sleep thereby. The number of those who rushed forward was so great, and there was such a press of them, that one penitentiary priest was not enough, and so they had to give him an assistant. Even that was not enough, for on Sunday, September 14, they celebrated an extraordinary jubilee with citywide processions, in which most of the turncoats took part. And after confessing into the ear of a priest, they returned to Belial's[2] Communion table.

[2]One of the names for the devil.

28

HUGUES SUREAU DU ROSIER

Confession of His Descent into Popery

1574

It is easy to assume that most Huguenot conversions were insincere and motivated solely by fear, but a number of Huguenots clearly did experience a severe crisis of belief as a result of the massacre, as minister Hugues Sureau Du Rosier's account of his own "descent into popery" suggests.

Although Du Rosier was just one of thousands of Huguenots who abjured in the wake of the massacre, his conversion was particularly damaging to the Huguenot cause because he was a minister and because he helped encourage others to recant as well. Catholic leaders brought him to Paris and used him to help convert the king of Navarre and prince of Condé. They also published a lengthy confession in which he attributed his conversion to a growing conviction that Catholicism must represent the true and universal faith because only it, and not the Protestant church, could trace its lineage directly back to Christ's apostles. Doubts about this belief continued to trouble Du Rosier, even after he recanted a second time and sought to return to the Reformed church, whose ministers kept him waiting more than a year before accepting a revised profession of faith in which he finally abandoned the idea of apos-

Hugues Sureau Du Rosier, *Confession et recognoissance, touchant sa cheute en la papauté et les horribles scandales par luy commis* (Basel, 1574), 6–7.

tolic succession in favor of doctrinal purity as the foundational principle on which the true church must rest. The following passage from the confession Du Rosier published on his return to Protestantism in 1574 shows how his convictions failed him under the stress of the massacre.

I was living in the Ile-de-France as pastor of a small church about a day's ride from Paris when, four days after learning of the massacre in that city, I decided to take refuge outside the kingdom. When I was leaving, in thinking about the difficulties I would have to face, I half decided to pretend to be a papist by wearing the insignia they wore on their hats and by my behavior and words, if the need arose. The following day, on my arrival in the first city on my route, I was asked who I was and found myself completely at a loss. I did not have the wits to say what I had planned and said something completely inappropriate, which made them suspicious of me. When the judge made me say under oath who I was, I freely confessed to everything. Being then put in prison, I resolved at first to endure whatever death they made me suffer and felt some peace in my conscience if I upheld the truth of the Gospel, which I was sure I would do, although my mind was in some turmoil because of certain thoughts I had concerning the apostolic succession in the Roman church. For this reason, I engaged in debates with some people who came to talk with me, and truth won out over lies. But this courage was just a puff of smoke, which did not last long, for when left alone I began to turn over in my mind the severity of the persecution that had just occurred, which I found quite different from preceding ones. I had always believed the past calamities to be so many visitations and rods by which God purged his church and had always judged them to be clear signs marking out the children of God. But inasmuch as that last [visitation] could be seen to entirely ruin the church, without the least sign of hope for its reestablishment, I began to see it as evidence of God's indignation, as if he had declared by this means that he detested and condemned the profession and exercise of our religion, seeing that he had struck us again and again, as if he wished entirely to ruin this church and favor instead the Roman one.

29

JOACHIM OPSER

Letter to the Abbot of Saint-Gall on Events in Paris

1572

The author of the following letter, Joachim Opser, was a young monk from the venerable abbey of Saint-Gall in Switzerland who was studying at the Jesuit college of Clermont in Paris when the massacre took place. When he learned that a friend serving in the king's Swiss Guard had been dispatched to carry news of the events to Switzerland, he hastened to send his own story of what he had seen and heard to his abbot at Saint-Gall. Opser first penned a very brief note, which merely related that, to "the Parisians' great joy," Admiral Coligny and other leading Huguenots had been "miserably massacred by order of the king." When he learned that his courier was not yet ready to depart, he added this more detailed account of events.

To Reverend Father in Christ, Lord Othmar, abbot of Saint-Gall in Switzerland,

Do not be astonished, reverend father, to receive two letters by the same courier. I wrote the first at the spur of the moment and sent it off in great haste because the bearer wanted to depart an hour later, but then, learning that his orders had been held up and his voyage consequently postponed, I took up my pen again, especially for a reason I shall indicate later on.

In the meantime, I want to transmit some details on these scenes that will give you a true pleasure, for I do not think it will bore you to tell you about how an event as unexpected as it is useful to our cause is developing and not only enrapturing the Christian world with admiration but also raising it to the summits of happiness. You will have heard all about it from the captain. Rejoice in advance, but do not, I beg you, despise or reject as superfluous that which I write you with

"Deux lettres de couvent à couvent, écrites de Paris pendant le massacre de la Saint-Barthélemy par Joachim Opser de Wyl," *Bulletin de la Société de l'histoire du Protestantisme français* 8 (1859): 287–89, 291–94.

perhaps more satisfaction than is seemly, because I affirm nothing except that which I have learned from trusted sources.

The admiral perished miserably on August 24 with all the heretic French nobility. This can be said without exaggeration—an immense carnage! I shuddered at the sight of that river full of naked and mutilated cadavers. To date, the king has spared only the king of Navarre. In fact, today, August 26, at about 1:00 P.M., the king of Navarre attended Mass with King Charles, giving everyone great hope of seeing him change religion. Condé's sons are being held captive by the king's order and are in great danger, for the king may punish these stubbornly opinionated champions of heresy as a lesson to others. Everyone agrees in praising the prudence and magnanimity of the king, who, after having by his goodness and indulgence fattened up, so to speak, the heretics like cattle, suddenly had their throats slit by his soldiers.

Clever Montgomery has escaped; Lord Méru the third son of the deceased constable [Anne de Montmorency], was captured with a number of others.[1] The Parisians anxiously await news of what the king will decide to do with him.

All of the heretic booksellers who have been caught have been massacred and thrown naked onto the waters. Ramus,[2] who was thrown out of the window of his upper-story bedroom, still lies naked on the shore, pierced by a number of dagger blows. In a word, there is no one (except maybe women) who is not killed or injured. . . .

The opinion of people of the better sort is that the kingdom of France will now regain its health, for after having defeated the leaders, it should be easy to get rid of the rest of the wicked ones. During this time, in the cemetery of the Holy Innocents, a hawthorn that has appeared dead for four years now has covered itself with flowers. I saw it with my own eyes. It is a sure sign that the true religion will be restored, and everyone is ardently embracing this omen. I piously held my rosary up to this hawthorn and touched it with it. . . .

Farewell. From Paris, August 26, 1572, at ten in the evening; from Paris, the abyss of heretics.

May heaven maintain you in good health, you and the community.

Brother Joachim Opser, humble student
P.S.: Next time, I'll write to everybody.

---

[1]Charles de Montmorency de Méru was not a Protestant but, like his brothers, a liberal Catholic who remained close to Coligny and other Protestant kinsmen.
[2]A distinguished university professor famous for his system of logic.

30

THE VENETIAN SENATE

Letter to the Venetian Ambassadors in France

1572

News of the massacre was greeted with joy by both the populace and the leaders of Catholic powers. As we have seen (Document 16), Venice's ambassadors in Paris kept the republic's rulers closely informed about what was happening in other European capitals. This response from the Venetian senate to the ambassadors' first dispatches about the Saint Bartholomew's Day Massacre clearly expresses the Venetian reaction to these events.

The event about which you have informed us at length in your letters of the 25th through 28th of the past month telling about the massacre of the heads and principal leaders of the Huguenot sect and the destruction of other adherents according to the order of His Serene Highness the king, not only in Paris but also in other parts of the kingdom, caused in us such joy as can rightly be born of something that has brought such notable benefits to Christianity, and in particular to the crown of the Most Christian King [Charles IX], among those who desire the success, prosperity, and grandeur of a prince so closely allied to our republic and held by us in such great esteem and consideration. We thus did not want to delay in demonstrating our contentment by sending you the present letter with the senate's concurrence. To this end, we have also organized a procession to give thanks to God.

Though confident that the two of you will not have failed to fulfill your duty in congratulating His Majesty, we nevertheless wanted to charge you to do so again in our name. You are to present him the attached letter, for which you will find here a copy, and to tell him that we rejoice immensely to see in him the courage that complements his singular goodness, great prudence, and virtue. We do not know by what action he could have better demonstrated this than by entirely

---

Giovanni Michiel and Sigismondo Cavalli, *La Saint-Barthélemy devant le Sénat de Venise*, ed. William Martin (Paris, 1872), 94–96.

destroying this plague so detrimental to his state and to the name of Christian, which his most serene predecessors, who have indeed earned the title of "Most Christian," have always defended with their lives. Since coming to the throne, His Majesty has similarly shown clear signs of his true piety and excellent virtue, such that today he has obtained, in keeping with the greatness of his courage and his good intentions, a most happy result in the very praiseworthy action through which he has succeeded in solidifying the foundations of the Catholic religion and reestablishing the obedience without which empires cannot for long endure. Because such a grand opportunity has opened to His Majesty to demonstrate to the world his holy thoughts directed toward beautiful actions and honorable enterprises, we are assured that he will continue to take all measures necessary to prevent such a pernicious seed from again taking root. We consider it certain that he will happily succeed, for, by the death of the chiefs, the members are scattered; and that excellent action on the part of His Most Serene Highness the king will thus live on, to his eternal glory, in the memory of men.

31

German Print of the Saint Bartholomew's Day Massacre

This print was made in Germany to publicize the horrors of the Saint Bartholomew's Day Massacre. Based on published accounts of the massacre, it simultaneously narrates the initial wounding of Admiral Coligny (center left), his being murdered in his bed (upper right), and his body being tossed from the window and mutilated in the street. Neither the artist nor the exact date of publication has been identified, but the engraving is in the style of other sixteenth-century illustrated news reports that circulated widely in the wake of important events. How does this image compare with that by François Dubois (Document 19)? What impression would it have made on viewers, and what details show where the artist's sympathies lay?

Political Responses

32

Protestant Resistance Theory: The Wake-Up Call for the French and Their Neighbors

1574

When they learned about the events of Saint Bartholomew's Day, French Protestants in La Rochelle refused obedience to the crown. They ceased paying taxes, denied entry to the royal army sent to make them submit, and welcomed the arrival of surviving Huguenot leaders who retreated to the city in the wake of the massacre. Charles IX's attempt to retake La Rochelle set off the fourth War of Religion. In contrast to the previous wars, the Huguenots did not attempt to frame this revolt as merely a limited protest against the king's ministers and certain of their policies. Instead, they boldly proclaimed their right to disobey, and even to take up arms against, a king who had violated fundamental rights belonging to the community. The Wake-Up Call for the French and Their Neighbors *offers a strong statement of this new theory of resistance.*

In the second of the two dialogues that make up the book (for the first, see Document 22), a pair of speakers, labeled simply the Historian and the Politician, assess the international situation and prospects of gaining support from abroad for France's beleaguered Huguenots. In this excerpt, the Politician explains why the Huguenots' rebellion is justified.

The Politician: First, it is necessary to establish this maxim: that there is only one infinite empire, that of all-powerful God, and consequently the power of any magistrate or prince is enclosed within certain limits and barriers beyond which the prince must not go nor the subject, if he does exceed them, obey. Otherwise, the empire of the magistrate would be made equal to that of the Sovereign Lord, a blasphemy too horrible even to consider. For even if

Le reveille-matin des françois, et de leurs voisins. Composé par Eusebe Philadelphe Cosmopolite, en forme de Dialogues (Edinburgh, 1574), 2:80–94.

the magistrate represents God's image, it is necessary to remember what God said to his prophet: I will not give my glory to another. Magistrates are thus established by God not so that in sharing his majesty they reserve for themselves a part of his glory, but so that as ministers and servants of the Lord, they return entirely to their master all glory and all honor.

Magistrates, if they do not take heed of their duty, can commit serious errors either in commanding that which goes against the first table of God's law or in forbidding that which is commanded by the first table.[1] Such commandments and prohibitions are profane and contrary to all piety. They offend also against the second table when they command that which cannot be done without violating the love due to one's neighbors or prohibit doing things that cannot be left undone without violating this same love, which must be kept inviolable, and such edicts must be considered iniquitous.

On this basis, that we owe only to God perfect obedience without exception, it follows that we must not on any account obey profane or iniquitous edicts of any magistrate or prince whatsoever, and consequently that subjects cannot in good conscience obey a king who commands things that are profane or iniquitous....

The question of whether we can in good conscience disobey profane and iniquitous edicts of magistrates, whoever they are, is thus resolved. It remains now to ask whether one can similarly in good conscience resist them, and for what reasons—it being surely more a question of resisting than of simply disobeying. Do not think that I thus favor the faction of furious and turbulent Anabaptists, whom we all admit can be properly chastised by the magistrate. Nor should one think that I advocate factious rebellion if I affirm that subjects are bound to resist, with arms if necessary, a magistrate who commands profane or iniquitous things. Resistance to the designs of a seditious magistrate is in truth a means of eliminating sedition and bringing about good order among the people.

So that the question may be more clearly treated and unraveled, I will first set forth several maxims as preludes to this fact.

First, that there is a mutual and reciprocal necessity and obligation between the magistrate and the subjects, as it is easy to recognize if one considers the origin, cause, and purposes of the institution of magistrates. It is certain that magistrates have been created for the

---

[1]The Ten Commandments were traditionally divided into two tables, the first containing obligations toward God and the second obligations toward other people.

people, and not the people for the magistrates; just as the tutor is created for the pupil and the shepherd for the flock, not the pupil for the tutor and the flock for the shepherd. There must thus have been some assemblies and groups of men before the creation of magistrates. One can still find people without magistrates, but no magistrate without people. It is thus the people who created the magistrate and not the magistrate the people. The latter, I say, created the first magistrates with a common agreement because of the need they felt for protection and for leadership.

People created princes for themselves so as to be governed in one fashion or another but nevertheless in such a way that the people always retained a goodly share of power and authority. One sees this in democratic states, in which those elected to office ask the advice and receive the voice of the people, not daring to order anything without their consent. These are called popular magistrates. Other people, preferring aristocratic government, have chosen and elected a certain number of the best of their citizens to whom they have committed all of the government of their state and public affairs. Still others, most valuing government by a single individual, have elected and raised someone above themselves to govern and lead them as monarch and sovereign. But never will a people be found who are so stupid and ill-advised as to have raised a magistrate onto their shoulders to whom they have given absolute power and authority to command regardless of what the people who chose him want. On the contrary, the people always, in submitting to the magistrate, bind and tie him to certain laws and conditions that he is not permitted to break or exceed. We see this still today in the establishment and coronation of kings, where they are asked to take a certain form of oath that they swear before being established, confining themselves in this way to the conditions that have been offered them. . . .

Having seen the origin and ways of creating magistrates, let us now consider the cause and reasons for which they have been created. We will find that it is nothing other than the good of the people, so that, as the Apostle says, the wicked live in awe and terror and the just in security and safety.

Aristotle said it very well in his *Politics*: Just as the pilot should have good navigation, the doctor the health of his patient, and the captain victory, so the king should have the good of his people and its safeguard always before his eyes. Moreover, the people having initially elected or in some other fashion raised the king to this end, and the king having pledged himself to it, when he deviates from it—when from being a good prince he becomes Charles IX; even when he simply places his own good above the public's, filling his coffers and increasing his revenues to the people's detriment— then the people's obligation is ended, and the people are freed from what they owed their king. No authority and government can be just and legitimate that is so centered on the king's own benefit that all public affairs in the kingdom are directed to it. . . .

These things having been set out, I return to the initial question: whether it is permissible to subjects to resist their magistrate, and how far does this freedom extend. But before beginning, it must be understood that subjects are not all of the same condition, for some are simply private subjects but others are called subjects only with respect to the sovereign magistrate. These are the lesser magistrates.

As to the question of whether the sovereign magistrate or king is so sovereign that only God is established above him, it seems that one can say that after God, the king is the first. I agree, but not absolutely, for, as I have already said, people have never been so stupid and ill-advised as to give anyone such a sovereign power without reserving for themselves, as it were, the reins of a strong and stout bridle, for fear that royalty, like a slippery road, should descend quickly into tyranny.

[He goes on to give specific examples of bodies that served to check the power of kings and even to depose them—Rome's senate, Sparta's ephors, the Holy Roman Empire's electors, England's Parliament, and, until the Valois kings destroyed it, France's Estates General.[2]]

Without doubt, those who have power to depose kings also have power to create them. Moreover, where this order is established, and certain persons are charged with bridling the power of kings and safeguarding the laws, these same people can and must resist

---

[2]An assembly comparable to England's Parliament with the right to consent to new taxes and to present grievances to the king but consisting of representatives of three "estates" (clergy, nobility, and commoners). The Estates General met only when called by the king, and this was less and less often after French kings gained the power to collect a regular head tax in the fourteenth century. By 1574, many French Protestants had lost confidence in the ability of the Estates General to protect their rights or limit royal authority. That is why the discussion shifts from the right to overthrow tyrants to the right to resist them.

any iniquitous or profane commandments on the part of the kings. They cannot let royalty and legitimate government degenerate into tyranny without manifestly betraying the people, who created these ranks largely for this very purpose of preventing tyranny. And if by misfortune tyranny occurs (as we, for our sins, witness now supremely, as properties and persons, honor and soul, are flouted at will), it is up to private subjects to seek remedy from the Estates, for certainly these three Estates stand as sovereign magistrates above the king in this respect, even if they are private and beneath the king in ordinary affairs.

[The Politician goes on to explain that the king has no right to proscribe the Estates and that any laws contrary to the well-being and rights of the people are invalid. But then another question arises: Can a part of the people resist if it believes itself seriously abused, even though its grievances have not been ratified as just by the people as a whole or by the Estates?]

After the aggrieved party has admonished its fellows and made clear to them their duty, if they refuse to listen, it is permitted by all human and divine law and reason not to overthrow the tyrant, even though he rightly should be overthrown, but rather to withdraw from his obedience and defend against the tyranny and violence of the one who, instead of being shepherd and father to the people, has become a brigand and thief. This can be done in good conscience and despite letting perish those who knowingly wish to perish, for it is in no way reasonable that my rights, my property, my honor, and my life—indeed my very salvation—should be abandoned and lost on account of the cowardice and disregard of others. . . .

[After hearing these arguments, the Historian expresses great relief and concludes that the Politician has fully justified the Huguenots' revolt.]

The Historian: Good Lord, but I am happy to have heard you set forth and explain so many good arguments to justify our brothers. They are more than sufficient to prove that La Rochelle and other oppressed cities and provinces (among which one might include all of France, from its four corners to its middle) are permitted [to refuse] obedience and submission to the tyrant, and at the very least to defend themselves against invasion by his henchmen, peculation by his officials, oppression by his tax collectors, and violence and debauchery on the part of his court. In a word, against all that proceeds from him and his Janissaries.[3]

And rather than them deserving to be called seditious for defending themselves or withdrawing obedience from the tyrant, on the contrary, the bad citizens, compatriots, and bad neighbors are those who fail to join them.

[3]The much-feared soldiers of the Ottoman emperor; by extension, troops and officials of a tyrannical king.

33

RICHARD VERSTEGAN

Horrible Cruelties of the Huguenots in France
1587

Richard Verstegan's Theater of the Cruelties of the Heretics of Our Time, *first published in Antwerp in 1587, helped internationalize the religious conflicts by bringing together images depicting the persecution of Catholics in England, France, and the Low Countries. This scene, one of twelve images illustrating atrocities allegedly committed by Protestants in France, shows Huguenot soldiers (A) disemboweling a man, (B) burying another man alive, (C) taking a sword to helpless infants, and (D) preparing to burn an already disemboweled man on a red-hot grate. The lines at the bottom read: "Never content, these senseless tyrants / Daily invent more new torments. / No suffering is great enough to appease their ardent wrath. / They delight in watching the poor innocents / They wrongly kill suffer cruel death, / And show by these torments their mortal hatred."*

Richard Verstegan, *Theatrum Crudelitatum Haereticorum Nostri Temporis* (Antwerp, 1587), 49. Bibliothèque nationale de France.

Horribles cruautez des Huguenots en France.

Ces Tirans insensez n'estants iamais contents,
Inuentent tous les iours autres nouueaux tourments,
A leur ardant couroux ne suffit nulle paine:
Ilz s'esgaient à voir souffrir cruelle mort
Aux pauures innocents, qu'ilz font mourir à tort,
Monstrant par tel tourments leur tant mortele haine.

143

34

HENRY IV

The Edict of Nantes

1598

The Saint Bartholomew's Day Massacre influenced the course of the Wars of Religion in contradictory ways. If it radicalized French Protestants in their abhorrence of a monarchy that could condone and even partici-pate in the murder of its subjects, it also radicalized many Catholics, who demanded that the wars continue unabated until the Protestant faith had been entirely annihilated in France. Other Catholics, however, were so appalled by the slaughter that they formed a new third party and called for a negotiated peace and a political end to the quarrels. Before the voices for peace could triumph, France endured another quarter century of civil and religious wars, during which time not only Protestants but also ardent Catholics revolted against the crown. Henry of Bourbon, king of Navarre, inherited the throne according to the traditional rules of suc-cession when the last Valois king, Henry III, died in 1589. As a Protes-tant, however, Henry was unacceptable to most French Catholics. Taking up arms to defeat the Holy League formed by Catholic radicals, Henry abjured his Protestant faith in 1593 so as to help win over his Catholic subjects. Paris opened its gates to him in 1594; many Holy League cities soon followed. The surrender of the last rebels in 1598 allowed Henry IV to turn at last from the battlefield to the problems of securing peace among his exhausted but still wary subjects.

Like earlier edicts of pacification, the Edict of Nantes, which set out the terms for civil peace in April 1598, represented a compromise between Protestant and Catholic demands. Once again, the Protestants had not been defeated on the battlefield. Indeed, they had helped Henry IV retake the league bastion of Amiens. He needed to respect his former coreligionists' demands for both security and the right to worship. At the same time, he needed to dissipate remaining sympathy for the league by reasserting the primacy of Catholicism throughout the kingdom and guaranteeing Catholics full freedom of worship, while limiting Protestant rights. In large measure, this was accomplished by piecing together

---

Edict du roy, & declaration sur les precedents edicts de pacification. Publié à Paris en Parlement, le xxvᵉ de Febvrier MDXCIX (Paris, 1599).

clauses, often verbatim, from previous edicts of pacification. The prologue, however, sets out Henry's more personal assessment of both what he and the kingdom had been through and what remained to be done.

Here is Henry's prologue, along with several of the first clauses of the edict. Why did the king frame the prologue so explicitly in terms of God's grace and will, and how might this have been received from a monarch whose religious conversion only five years earlier was still fresh in his subjects' minds?

Henry, by the Grace of God king of France and Navarre. To all present and to come.

Greetings.

Among the infinite mercies that it has pleased God to bestow upon us, the most signal and remarkable is to have given us the virtue and strength not to yield to the frightful troubles, confusions, and disorders that prevailed on our accession to this kingdom, which was divided in so many parts and factions that the most legitimate was just about the smallest, and to have nevertheless so strengthened us against this turmoil that we have finally overcome it and have now reached a safe and restful harbor for this state. For which to him alone is due the glory and to us the thankfulness and indebtedness that he has chosen to make use of our efforts to achieve this good work, in which it has been visible to all that we have not only done that which was our duty and in our power but something more, which might not perhaps under other circumstances have been appropriate to the dignity which we hold, and which we no longer fear to expose because we have so often and so freely exposed our own life.

And not being able, in this great concurrence of such important and perilous affairs, to resolve them all at once and at the same time, it has been necessary to order things such that we first undertook those that could not be resolved except by force and put off for some time the others that could and should be resolved through reason and justice, such as the broader differences among our good subjects and the particular ills of the healthiest parts of the state, which we believe can be more easily cured after having removed their principal cause, the continuation of civil war. And having by the grace of God well and happily succeeded in this, fighting and hostilities having entirely ceased throughout the kingdom, we hope that he will favor us as well in the other affairs that remain to be settled and that, by this means, we will arrive at the establishment of the good peace and tranquil repose that has always been the goal of all of our hopes and intentions and the reward that we desire for having endured so many pains and hardships in the course of our life.

Among the affairs that have required patience, one of the principal ones has been the complaints that we have received from several of our Catholic provinces and cities that the exercise of the Catholic religion has not been universally reestablished, as is required by the edicts previously issued for the pacification of the troubles caused by religion; but also the supplications and remonstrances that have been made to us by our subjects of the so-called Reformed religion concerning both the nonfulfillment of what has been promised them by the edicts and what they desire in addition for the exercise of their religion, the freedom of their consciences, and the security of their persons and fortunes, presuming as they do to have just cause for new and greater apprehensions on account of these last troubles and commotions, whose principal purpose and basis has been their ruin. In order not to take on too much at one time and also so that the furor of battle should not affect the establishment of laws, however good they might be, we have continually put off seeing to these things. But now that it has pleased God to allow us to begin to enjoy some greater repose, we have thought that it could not be better employed than in seeing to that which concerns the glory of his holy name and service and ensuring that he can be adored and worshipped by all of our subjects. And if it has not yet pleased him to permit this to be in one and the same form and religion, at least may it be with a common intention and rule so that there is no trouble or turmoil among them on this account, and we and this kingdom can continue to merit and preserve the glorious title of Most Christian, which has for such a long time and so deservedly been earned, and by the same means remove the root of the problems and troubles that can occur on account of religion, which are the trickiest and most penetrating of all.

For this reason, having recognized these affairs to be of great importance and worthy of most serious consideration, after having reviewed again the grievance petitions of our Catholic subjects and also permitted our subjects of the so-called Reformed religion to call together representatives to draw up and bring together all of their remonstrances, and having conferred with them multiple times for this purpose and reviewed the preceding edicts, we have judged it necessary to now give all of our subjects a clear, sound, and absolute general law by which all of the differences that have previously arisen among them and might hereafter arise may be regulated and both sides contented, as far as the times allow. Having for our part entered into these deliberations only on account of the zeal that we have for God's service and so that our subjects may in the future render such service and establish among themselves a good and enduring peace.

To this end, we implore and expect from his divine goodness the same protection and favor that he has always visibly shown this kingdom from its beginnings and throughout the great age it has acquired. May he grant our subjects the grace to understand that after their duty to God and to us, the principal foundation of their union and concord, tranquillity and repose, and the reestablishment of this entire country in its original splendor, opulence, and strength rests in observing this our law. And for our part, we promise to see that it is strictly observed without allowing it to be violated in any way.

35

HENRY IV

Speech to the Magistrates of the Parlement of Paris

1599

Royal edicts went into effect only after being registered in the king's sovereign courts, and the parlements sometimes deliberately withheld registration as a way of expressing opposition to royal policies. They did this with the Edict of Nantes, which many magistrates believed made too many concessions to the Protestants. While the parlements delayed, Catholic preachers in Paris and other cities fomented more opposition to the edict. To cut short these protests, Henry IV called the magistrates of the Parlement of Paris before him in January 1599 and delivered the following speech. The edict was registered six weeks later.

Pierre de l'Estoile, *Mémories-journaux de Pierre de L'Estoile,* ed. Petitot. 4 vols. Collection complète des mémories relatifs à l'histoire de France, vol. 47 (Paris, 1825), 3:243–44.

You see me here in my study, where I have come to speak to you, not dressed in royal robes, nor wearing sword and cape, like my predecessors, nor as a prince who comes to meet with foreign ambassadors, but dressed like the father of a family, in his doublet, to speak frankly to his children. What I have to tell you is that I pray you to register the edict which I have given to those of the Protestant religion. What I have done is for the sake of peace. I have made it abroad; I wish it also in my kingdom. You must obey me, if only in consideration for my rank and the obligation that all of my subjects have toward me, and particularly all of you members of my Parlement. I have given some of you back their homes, from which they were banished, and others their faith, which they no longer had.[1] If obedience was due to my predecessors, it is owed with more devotion to me, inasmuch as I have reestablished the state. God chose me to put me into this kingdom, which is mine by inheritance and by acquisition. The members of my Parlement would no longer hold their offices without me. Those who prevent my edict from passing want war. I will declare it against the Protestants tomorrow, but I will not wage it; I will send them instead.

I have made this edict, and I want it observed. My will alone should serve as reason; in an obedient state, no one ever asks the king for a reason. I am king now and speak to you as a king; I wish to be obeyed.

---

[1] Members of the Parlement of Paris who sided with the crown against the Holy League were forced to flee Paris during the league's takeover of that city. They established a separate court in Tours and returned to Paris only after Henry IV's victory over the league, at which point he required the returning magistrates and those who had stayed in Paris to merge into a single court despite the hard feelings that remained on both sides.

5

Memories of the Massacre

36

MICHEL DE MONTAIGNE

Apology for Raymond Sebond

1588

*Born of a noble family and trained as a jurist, Michel de Montaigne
(1533–1592) witnessed the ravages of the Wars of Religion firsthand in
his native Bordelais. Retiring at the age of thirty-eight from his position
as a counselor in the Parlement of Bordeaux, Montaigne began his true
life's work, which was a series of essays in which he explored the principles by which he and others should live. "I am myself the matter of my
book," he wrote, and yet he found that he could not write about himself
without asking bigger questions about what it means to be human and
what we can and cannot know for certain. The following passage is taken
from one of his most famous essays, "Apology for Raymond Sebond."
Largely written between 1575 and 1580, the essay probes the limits of
human reason but also shows how the turmoil of the Wars of Religion
influenced Montaigne's thought, making him skeptical about human
motivations and behavior, especially when people claimed to act in the
name of religious truth. Although Montaigne remained a practicing
Catholic, his family was religiously divided, and he did not choose to
remain in the church of his ancestors without giving the matter a great
deal of thought. What arguments does Montaigne offer for his decision to*

Michel de Montaigne, "Apology for Raymond Sebond," in *The Complete Essays*, ed. and
trans. Donald M. Frame (Stanford, Calif.: Stanford University Press, 1958), 323–25, 436.
The basic text here is the 1588 edition of the essays, but some post-1588 additions were
included by Frame.

stay in the Catholic Church? How did his recognition that this decision was ultimately based on human reasons pave the way for greater religious toleration?

Let us confess the truth: if anyone should sift out of the army, even the average loyalist army, those who march in it from the pure zeal of affection for religion, and also those who consider only the protection of the laws of their country or the service of their prince, he could not make up one complete company of men-at-arms out of them. Whence comes this, that there are so few who have maintained the same will and the same pace in our public movements, and that we see them now going only at a walk, now riding with free rein, and the same men now spoiling our affairs by their violence and asperity, now by their coolness, sluggishness, and heaviness, if it is not that they are driven to it by private and accidental considerations according to whose diversity they are stirred?

I see this evident, that we willingly accord to piety only the services that flatter our passions. There is no hostility that excels Christian hostility. Our zeal does wonders when it is seconding our leaning toward hatred, cruelty, ambition, avarice, detraction, rebellion. Against the grain, toward goodness, benignity, moderation, unless as by a miracle some rare nature bears it, it will neither walk nor fly.

Our religion is made to extirpate vices; it covers them, fosters them, incites them.

We must not give God chaff for wheat, as they say. If we believed in him, I do not say by faith, but with a simple belief; in fact (and I say it to our great confusion), if we believed in him just as in any other history, if we knew him like one of our comrades, we would love him above all other things, for the infinite goodness and beauty that shines in him. At least he would march in the same rank in our affection as riches, pleasures, glory, and our friends.

The best of us does not fear to outrage him as he fears to outrage his neighbor, his kinsman, his master. . . .

All this is a very evident sign that we receive our religion only in our own way and with our own hands, and not otherwise than as other religions are received. We happen to have been born in a country where it was in practice; or we regard its antiquity or the authority of the men who have maintained it; or we fear the threats it fastens upon unbelievers, or pursue its promises. Those considerations should be employed in our belief, but as subsidiaries; they are human ties. Another region, other witnesses, similar promises and threats, might imprint upon us in the same way a contrary belief.

We are Christians by the same title that we are Perigordians or Germans. . . .

Truth must have one face, the same and universal. If man knew any rectitude and justice that had body and real existence, he would not tie it down to the condition of the customs of this country or that. It would not be from the fancy of the Persians or the Indians that virtue would take its form.

There is nothing subject to more continual agitation than the laws. Since I was born I have seen those of our neighbors the English change three or four times; not only in political matters, in which people want to dispense with constancy, but in the most important subject that can be, to wit, religion. At which I am shamed and vexed, the more so because that is a nation with which the people of my region formerly had such intimate acquaintance that there still remain in my house some traces of our old cousinship.

And here at home I have seen things which were capital offenses among us become legitimate; and we who consider other things legitimate are liable, according to the uncertainty of the fortunes of war, to be one day guilty of human and divine high treason, when our justice falls into the mercy of injustice, and, after a few years of captivity, assumes a contrary character.

How could that ancient god [Apollo] more clearly accuse human knowledge of ignorance of the divine being, and teach men that religion was only a creature of their own invention, suitable to bind their society together, than by declaring, as he did, to those who sought instruction therein at his tripod, that the true cult for each man was that which he found observed, according to the practice of the place he was in?

37

VOLTAIRE

The Philosophical Dictionary on Fanaticism
1764

Among the first—and most enduringly famous—proponents of the new way of thinking that came to be known as the Enlightenment was François-Marie Arouet, better known by his pen name, Voltaire (1694–1778). A brilliant satirist, Voltaire first wrote for the stage but soon turned to critical essays, novellas, and other media that allowed him to season social criticism with appealing wit. This passage from the Philosophical Dictionary *he published in 1764 uses the events of Saint Bartholomew's Day to denounce the effects of religious fanaticism.*

Fanaticism is to superstition what delirium is to fever and rage to anger. The man visited by ecstasies and visions, who takes dreams for realities and his fancies for prophecies, is an enthusiast; the man who supports his madness with murder is a fanatic. Juan Diaz, in retreat at Nuremberg, was firmly convinced that the pope was the Antichrist of the Apocalypse, and that he bore the sign of the beast; he was merely an enthusiast; his brother, Bartholomew Diaz, who came from Rome to assassinate his brother out of piety, and who did in fact kill him for the love of God, was one of the most abominable fanatics ever raised up by superstition.[1]

[1]Juan Diaz, from Cuenca, Spain, was murdered by his brother Alfonso (not Bartholomew, as Voltaire had it), a chamberlain to the pope, on March 17, 1546. Converted to Protestantism while a student in Paris, Juan Diaz traveled to Geneva, where he was well received by Calvin, and then set off to visit Protestant churches in Germany. A Spanish priest he met, having failed to reconvert him, alerted Diaz's brother Alfonso, who came to find him and, having also tried but failed to reconvert him, murdered him in his bed. Calvin published a pamphlet about the murder in 1546 to "alert the faithful how the Church of God is subject to many persecutions," so that they could steel themselves in courage and constancy. The pamphlet has been reprinted by Francis Higman, "Calvin, Le polar et la propagande: L'histoire d'un meurtre execrable," *Bibliothèque d'Humanisme et Renaissance*, 54 (1992): 111–23.

Voltaire, *Philosophical Dictionary*, trans. Peter Gay (New York: Basic Books, 1962), 267–69.

Polyeucte, who goes to the temple on a solemn holiday to knock over and smash the statues and ornaments, is a less dreadful but no less ridiculous fanatic than Diaz.[2] The assassins of the duke François de Guise, of William, prince of Orange, of king Henri III, of king Henri IV, and of so many others, were fanatics sick with the same mania as Diaz.

The most detestable example of fanaticism was that of the burghers of Paris who on St. Bartholomew's Night went about assassinating and butchering all their fellow citizens who did not go to mass, throwing them out of windows, cutting them in pieces.

There are cold-blooded fanatics: such as judges who condemn to death those who have committed no other crime than failing to think like them; and these judges are all the more guilty, all the more deserving of the execration of mankind, since, unlike Clément, Châtel, Ravaillac, Damiens,[3] they were not suffering from an attack of insanity; surely they should have been able to listen to reason.

Once fanaticism has corrupted a mind, the malady is almost incurable. . . .

The only remedy for this epidemic malady is the philosophical spirit which, spread gradually, at last tames men's habits and prevents the disease from starting; for, once the disease has made any progress, one must flee and wait for the air to clear itself. Laws and religion are not strong enough against the spiritual pest; religion, far from being healthy food for infected brains, turns to poison in them. These miserable men have forever in their minds the example of Ehud, who assassinated King Eglon; of Judith, who cut off Holofernes' head while she was sleeping with him; of Samuel, who chopped king Agag in pieces. They cannot see that these examples which were respectable in antiquity are abominable at the present; they borrow their frenzies from the very religion that condemns them.

Even the law is impotent against these attacks of rage; it is like reading a court decree to a raving maniac. These fellows are certain

---

[2]Polyeuctos was an early Christian saint—by tradition a Roman army officer martyred in Armenia under Valerian because he first tore up an edict requiring everyone to worship idols and then, meeting a procession carrying twelve idols through the streets, dashed them to the ground and broke them. The French dramatist Pierre Corneille wrote a play about Polyeuctos in 1642.

[3]Jacques Clément assassinated Henry III in 1589; Jean Châtel tried to kill Henry IV in 1594; François Ravaillac succeeded in killing him in 1610; Robert-François Damiens attempted but failed to kill Louis XV in 1757.

that the holy spirit with which they are filled is above the law, that their enthusiasm is the only law they must obey.

What can we say to a man who tells you that he would rather obey God than men, and that therefore he is sure to go to heaven for butchering you?

Ordinarily fanatics are guided by rascals, who put the dagger into their hands; these latter resemble the Old Man of the Mountain who is supposed to have made imbeciles taste the joys of paradise and who promised them an eternity of pleasures of which he had given them a foretaste, on condition that they assassinated all those he would name to them. There is only one religion in the world that has never been sullied by fanaticism, that of the Chinese men of letters. The schools of philosophers were not only free from this pest, they were its remedy; for the effect of philosophy is to make the soul tranquil, and fanaticism is incompatible with tranquility. If our holy religion has so often been corrupted by this infernal delirium, it is the madness of men which is at fault.

38

COORDINATING COMMITTEE FOR THE CHARTER FOR LIVING TOGETHER

Message to His Holiness Pope John Paul II
1997

In the spring of 1997, Vatican spokesmen announced the schedule for the World Youth Day celebrations to be held that summer in Paris. The international gathering was to close with an immense outdoor Mass on Sunday, August 24. French Protestants, upset because the date coincided with the 425th anniversary of the Saint Bartholomew's Day Massacre, seized on the occasion to ask the pope explicitly to call to memory the massacre when he addressed the World Youth Day gathering. They also asked him to join with them in condemning more recent examples of religious and

"Charte du vivre ensemble: Jeunes croyants de religions différentes, Ensemble pour l'avenir" and "Message à sa Sainteté le Pape Jean-Paul II." © Fédération Protestante de France, 1997, http://www.protestants.org/docpro/doc/0168.htm and http://www.protestants.org/docpro/doc/0699.htm (accessed March 25, 2008).

ethnic hatred. The following letter and Charter for Living Together, drafted by a committee operating out of the Federation of French Protestants' Youth Department, were sent to Pope John Paul II on May 25, 1997. When the charter was made public three days later, it had already gained the support of the Jewish Federation of France, the Great Mosque of Paris, the World Fellowship of Orthodox Youth, and the Union of French Buddhists, among other organizations.

MAY 25, 1997

Holy Father,

August 24, 1997, will mark the end of the 12th World Youth Days. August 24 is also Saint Bartholomew's Day, which, in France, still evokes for many the bloody event of 1572 when religious intolerance and politics led to the well-known massacre.

Now that you invite world youth to prepare for the jubilee of the year 2000, we ask you to recall this tragedy to mind and to associate with it much more recent dramas: Algeria, Burundi, Ireland, Rwanda, Sudan, Tibet, Yugoslavia, Zaire. . . .

Today still, political and religious intolerance divides; it oppresses; it kills.

More than ever, we need to learn to live together with respect for our differences and the division in our convictions.

That is why we want to send you this charter. It has been signed by young people from different faiths. It testifies to a strong wish to construct our future together.

A true pact of tolerance, we affirm there together both the convictions strongly anchored in our respective beliefs and the need to know one another better so as to better understand and share with one another.

We ask you to please reserve a favorable welcome for our charter and to carry into your ministry the aspirations it expresses. Is it possible that you might give evidence of your support by signing this charter? This could be the occasion for an interfaith encounter within the context of the 12th World Youth Days.

We hope that the youth of the Catholic Church will associate itself with this charter; we can thus proceed together toward the next millennium, strengthened by what already unites us and respectful of our differences.

Please accept, Most Holy Father, the homage of our profound respect.

Charter for Living Together

YOUNG BELIEVERS OF DIFFERENT RELIGIONS,
TOGETHER FOR THE FUTURE

MAY 1997

This August 24, 1997, at the end of the 12th World Youth Days organized by the Roman Catholic Church, we, young people belonging to
different religions, affirm our wish to live together and united to enter
into the next millennium.

This unity must be founded on a true pact of tolerance.

We recognize that there is not a single Youth but rather youths, as
there are multiple ways of living one's spirituality.

We affirm that in order to live together, it is best to know and
understand one another. It is also best to listen to one another so as to
give one another the best reception.

We wish to live together by sharing our differences so as to enrich
our future projects.

We wish to share the spiritual riches that are ours.

We affirm the urgency of building together our future on confidence, fraternity, and solidarity rather than on mistrust, hatred, and
withdrawal into ourselves. Also, we wish to pledge ourselves to a more
just and brotherly world.

We believe that the dramas that buffet our world are not the prod-
uct of fate. We have a share in responsibility for them.

The future of this world depends equally on our individual and col-
lective undertakings.

This is why we wish to take action against any form of ideology of
exclusion, fundamentalist intransigence, and fanaticism, [which are]
sources of violence and injustice, by joining together our energies and
values.

Strengthened by what already unites us and respectful of our differences, we invite youths of all countries, of all religious families and
confessions, to join with us.

[signed] The Coordinating Committee for the Charter for Living
Together

*[A list of more than twenty Protestant, Catholic, Jewish, Muslim, and
Eastern Orthodox organizations, collectively representing more than
300,000 young people, follows.]*

39

POPE JOHN PAUL II

Address to World Youth Day Celebrants

August 23, 1997

Vatican officials did not initially acknowledge the letter from the Coordinating Committee for the Charter for Living Together (Document 38), prompting the committee to send a second letter on August 21. But the archbishop of Paris, Cardinal Jean-Marie Lustiger,[1] and the head of the French Bishops' Conference invited Protestants to join them in a prayer vigil intended as a time for memory and reconciliation on August 19, just prior to World Youth Day, in the church of Saint-Germain l'Auxerrois. They also announced their intention of taking up the task of memory, as the pope had called for them to do in preparation for the new millennium, by looking more critically into past silences and omissions on the part of the Catholic Church. John Paul II associated himself with these efforts in the following address, which he made to the World Youth Day audience on August 23, 1997. How well does the pope's address respond to the issues raised by the Charter for Living Together?

On the eve of 24 August we cannot forget the sad Massacre of Saint Bartholomew's Day, an event of very obscure causes in the political and religious history of France. Christians did things which the Gospel condemns. If I speak of the past, it is because "acknowledging the weaknesses of the past is an act of honesty and courage which helps us to strengthen our faith, which alerts us to face today's temptations and

---

[1]Born into a Jewish family in Paris, Aaron Lustiger (1926–2007) was converted to Catholicism and took the name Jean-Marie when his parents sent him into hiding during the Nazi occupation. Ordained in 1954, Lustiger worked to improve Jewish-Christian relations as he rose in the church and encouraged its leaders to face up to some of the darker parts of its past.

"World Youth Day, 1997, Greetings of the Holy Father, Vigil, August 23, 1997," CIOFS LIST, SFO International Council, September 1997, http://www.ciofs.org/per/1997/lc97en38.htm (accessed March 25, 2008).

challenges and prepares us to meet them." Therefore I willingly support the initiatives of the French bishops, for, with them, I am convinced that only forgiveness, offered and received, leads little by little to a fruitful dialogue, which will in turn ensure a fully Christian reconciliation. Belonging to different religious traditions must not constitute today a source of opposition and tension. Quite the contrary, our common love for Christ impels us to seek tirelessly the path of full unity.

A Chronology
of the Religious Conflicts in France
(1517–1598)

1517 Martin Luther posts Ninety-five Theses challenging the practice of indulgences.

1521 Luther is condemned as a heretic; the Sorbonne bans his writings in France.

1535 King Francis I steps up persecution of heresy; Calvin and other converts flee France.

1550s First French Reformed churches are founded.

1559 Henry II makes peace with Spain and is killed during a tournament celebrating the peace.

1560 *March*: Protestants attempt to seize King Francis II at Amboise.

December: Francis II dies; Catherine de Medici becomes regent for King Charles IX.

1561 *April*: Catherine issues an edict allowing limited toleration for Protestants.

Huguenots begin to seize churches in the South; violent incidents increase.

1562 *January*: Royal edict allows limited right to worship for Protestants.

March: Massacre of Vassy sets off first War of Religion.

1563 *February*: Francis, duke of Guise, is killed.

March: Peace of Amboise ends first War of Religion.

1567 *September*: Huguenots attempt to seize Charles IX at Meaux; the second War of Religion begins.

1568 *March*: Peace of Longjumeau ends the second War of Religion.

August: Third War of Religion breaks out.

Ordinances of Saint-Maur forbid Protestant worship.

1569 Louis of Bourbon, prince of Condé, is killed at the Battle of Jarnac; Admiral Coligny is executed in effigy.

1570 *August*: Peace of Saint-Germain ends the third War of Religion.

1571 *December*: Cross of Gastines riots disturb the peace in Paris.

1572 *August 18*: Henry of Bourbon, king of Navarre, weds Marguerite of Valois.

August 22: Assassin attempts to kill Coligny.

August 24: Saint Bartholomew's Day Massacre begins.

Fourth War of Religion breaks out.

1573 *June*: Peace of La Rochelle ends the fourth War of Religion, but the south remains in rebellion.

1574 *February*: Fifth War of Religion begins.

May: Charles IX dies; Catherine de Medici is regent again until Henry III returns to France.

1576 *February*: Henry of Navarre escapes from court and returns to Protestantism.

May: Peace of Beaulieu, ending the fifth War of Religion, favors the Protestants; Catholic radicals form the Holy League.

December: Sixth War of Religion breaks out.

1580 Seventh War of Religion is fought in southern France.

1584 *June*: Francis, duke of Anjou, dies, leaving Henry of Navarre heir to the throne; the Holy League is revived.

1585 *July*: Henry III submits to pressure from the league and forbids Protestant worship.

1586 Henry III allies with the league to make war on the Huguenots.

1588 *May*: Holy League seizes power in Paris and drives out Henry III.

December: Henry III orders Henry, duke of Guise, killed.

1589 *April*: Henry III makes an alliance with Henry of Navarre.

August: Henry III is assassinated; Henry of Navarre claims the throne as Henry IV and fights to take Paris.

1593 *July*: Henry IV converts to Catholicism.

1594 *March*: Paris opens its gates to Henry IV; many other Holy League cities follow.

1598 Last league holdouts surrender.

April: Edict of Nantes sets out terms of toleration for the Huguenots.

May: Peace is made with Spain, which aided the Holy League.

Questions for Consideration

1. How did Protestants and Catholics caricature each other for propaganda purposes? Consider the manipulation of theological differences as well as blunter tactics such as sexual slander. (See in particular Documents 1–3.)

2. Why were both Protestants and Catholics able to interpret the public burning of condemned heretics as a validation of their beliefs? (See Documents 4–6.)

3. Why did Catherine de Medici's strategy of granting Protestants a limited right to assemble for worship miscarry? Were there better alternatives that she might have adopted? (See Documents 8–11.)

4. What sorts of events or activities were most likely to spark outright violence between Protestant and Catholic groups even before the Wars of Religion broke out? What can you infer from these documents about who was most likely to commit acts of religious violence and why? (See Documents 8–11.)

5. How did the violence that took place during the Saint Bartholomew's Day Massacre echo earlier incidents of religious violence, and how did it differ? How might we explain the differences? What, in your opinion, was most responsible for people's willingness to go beyond previous limits in attacking the Huguenots?

6. How do Protestant and Catholic accounts of the religious conflicts differ in the roles they attribute to women in the Reformed faith? How might we explain these differences?

7. How should we understand the king's role in the Saint Bartholomew's Day Massacre, given the contradictory explanations he offered for it? Does it matter in the end whether he ordered the assassination of the Huguenot leaders or whether this was done without his orders or consent? Why, or why not? (See Documents 22, 23, and 32.)

8. Why did many people blame Catherine de Medici for the decision to kill the Huguenot leadership? Would such a decision have been consistent with her previous policies concerning the Huguenots? If not, what might explain such a change in policy? (See especially Document 16.)

161

9. Why do you think massacres occurred in only some provincial cities? What conditions seem to have been conducive to maintaining the peace, and what conditions seem to have created inflammatory situations? (See Documents 24–26.)

10. What role did city officials and local militias appear to play in the massacre? On balance, do you think they did more to keep the peace or to disturb it and why? Consider provincial cases as well as that of Paris.

11. What impact did the massacre have on the surviving Huguenot population in France and why? What, beyond simple fear, motivated the many conversions that took place in the wake of the massacre? (See Documents 27 and 28.)

12. How did Catholics both in France and abroad justify the joy they often expressed immediately after the massacre? Why was this sentiment short-lived? (See especially Documents 29 and 30.)

13. How did French Protestants justify resistance to royal authority in the wake of the massacre? What was new about these arguments, and what impact did they have? (See Document 32.)

14. Why did Henry IV have to force his Parlement to register the Edict of Nantes? What does this tell us about the religious situation in France in 1598? (See Documents 34 and 35.)

15. How did the conclusions Michel de Montaigne drew from France's religious conflicts open the way for greater religious toleration? (See Document 36.)

16. Writing during the Enlightenment, Voltaire evoked the Saint Bartholomew's Day Massacre as a way of condemning superstition and fanaticism (Document 37). More recently, the massacre has been used to epitomize the dangers of both political and religious intolerance. How effective are these analogies? What underlying mental structures or attitudes does the massacre have in common with the "more recent dramas" referred to in Document 38?

Selected Bibliography

Baumgartner, Frederic J. *France in the Sixteenth Century.* New York: St. Martin's Press, 1995.

Benedict, Philip. *Christ's Churches Purely Reformed: A Social History of Calvinism.* New Haven, Conn.: Yale University Press, 2002.

———. *Graphic History: The Wars, Massacres and Troubles of Tortorel and Perrissin.* Geneva: Droz, 2007.

———. *Rouen during the Wars of Religion.* Cambridge: Cambridge University Press, 1981.

———. "The Saint Bartholomew's Massacres in the Provinces." *Historical Journal* 21, no. 2 (1978): 205–25.

Benedict, Philip, Lawrence M. Bryant, and Kristen B. Neuschel. "Graphic History: What Readers Knew and Were Taught in the *Quarante Tableaux* of Perrissin and Tortorel." *French Historical Studies* 28 (Spring 2005): 175–229.

Benedict, Philip, et al., eds. *Reformation, Revolt and Civil War in France and the Netherlands, 1555–1585.* Amsterdam: Royal Netherlands Academy of Arts and Sciences, 1999.

Bouwsma, William. *John Calvin: A Sixteenth Century Portrait.* New York: Oxford University Press, 1988.

Carroll, Stuart. "The Guise Affinity and Popular Protest during the Wars of Religion." *French History* 9 (1995): 121–51.

———. *Noble Power during the French Wars of Religion: The Guise Affinity and the Catholic Cause in Normandy.* Cambridge: Cambridge University Press, 1998.

Cottret, Bernard. *Calvin: A Biography.* Translated by M. Wallace McDonald. Grand Rapids, Mich.: Eerdmans, 2000.

Crouzet, Denis. *Les guerriers de Dieu: La violence au temps des troubles de religion.* 2 vols. Seyssel, France: Champ Vallon, 1990.

Davis, Natalie Zemon. *Society and Culture in Early Modern France: Eight Essays.* Stanford, Calif.: Stanford University Press, 1975.

Diefendorf, Barbara B. *Beneath the Cross: Catholics and Huguenots in Sixteenth-Century Paris.* Oxford: Oxford University Press, 1991.

———. "The Religious Wars in France." In *A Companion to the Reformation World*, edited by R. Po-chia Hsia, 150–68. Oxford: Blackwell, 2004.

————. "Simon Vigor: A Radical Preacher in Sixteenth-Century France." *Sixteenth Century Journal* 18, no. 3(1987): 399–410.

Evenett, H. Outram. *The Cardinal of Lorraine and the Council of Trent: A Study in the Counter-Reformation.* Cambridge: Cambridge University Press, 1930.

Franklin, Julian H., ed. and trans. *Constitutionalism and Resistance in the Sixteenth Century: Three Treatises by Hotman, Beza, and Mornay.* New York: Pegasus, 1969.

Greengrass, Mark. "The Anatomy of a Religious Revolt in Toulouse in May 1562." *Journal of Ecclesiastical History* 34 (1983): 367–91.

Gregory, Brad S. *Salvation at Stake: Christian Martyrdom in Early Modern Europe.* Cambridge, Mass.: Harvard University Press, 1999.

Harding, Robert R. "The Mobilization of Confraternities against the Reformation in France." *Sixteenth Century Journal* 11, no. 2 (1980): 85–107.

Heller, Henry. *The Conquest of Poverty: The Calvinist Revolt in Sixteenth-Century France.* Leiden: Brill, 1986.

Holt, Mack P. *The French Wars of Religion, 1562–1629.* 2nd ed. Cambridge: Cambridge University Press, 2005.

————. "Putting Religion Back into the Wars of Religion." *French Historical Studies* 18 (1993): 524–51.

Kaplan, Benjamin J. *Divided by Faith: Religious Conflict and the Practice of Toleration in Early Modern Europe.* Cambridge, Mass.: Harvard University Press, 2007.

Kelley, Donald R. *François Hotman: A Revolutionary's Ordeal.* Princeton, N.J.: Princeton University Press, 1973.

Kingdon, Robert M. *Geneva and the Coming of the Wars of Religion in France, 1555–1563.* Geneva: Droz, 1956.

————. *Geneva and the Consolidation of the Wars of Religion in France, 1564–72.* Geneva: Droz, 1967.

————. *Myths about the St. Bartholomew's Day Massacres, 1572–1576.* Cambridge, Mass.: Harvard University Press, 1988.

Knecht, Robert J. *Catherine de' Medici.* London: Longman, 1998.

————. *The French Civil Wars.* Harlow, Eng.: Longman, 2000.

Konnert, Mark W. *Local Politics in the French Wars of Religion: The Towns of Champagne, the Duc de Guise, and the Catholic League, 1560–95.* Aldershot, Eng.: Ashgate, 2006.

Luria, Keith P. *Sacred Boundaries: Religious Coexistence and Conflict in Early-Modern France.* Washington, D.C.: Catholic University of America Press, 2005.

Monter, William. *Judging the French Reformation: Heresy Trials by Sixteenth-Century Parlements.* Cambridge, Mass.: Harvard University Press, 1999.

Potter, David, ed. and trans. *The French Wars of Religion: Selected Documents.* New York: St. Martin's Press, 1997.

Racaut, Luc. *Hatred in Print: Catholic Propaganda and Protestant Identity during the French Wars of Religion*. Aldershot, Eng.: Ashgate, 2002.

Roberts, Penny. *A City in Conflict: Troyes during the French Wars of Religion*. Manchester, Eng.: Manchester University Press, 1996.

Salmon, J. H. M. *The French Religious Wars in English Political Thought*. Oxford: Oxford University Press, 1959.

———. *Society in Crisis: France in the Sixteenth Century*. New York: St. Martin's Press, 1975.

Shepardson, Nikki. *Burning Zeal: The Rhetoric of Martyrdom and the Protestant Community in Reformation France, 1520–1570*. Bethlehem, Pa.: Lehigh University Press, 2007.

Smither, James R. "The St. Bartholomew's Day Massacre and Images of Kingship in France: 1572–1574." *Sixteenth Century Journal* 22, no. 1 (1991): 27–46.

Soman, Alfred. *The Massacre of St. Bartholomew: Reappraisals and Documents*. The Hague: Martinus Nijhoff, 1974.

Sutherland, N. M. *The Huguenot Struggle for Recognition*. New Haven, Conn.: Yale University Press, 1980.

———. *The Massacre of St. Bartholomew and the European Conflict, 1559–1572*. London: Macmillan, 1973.

———. *Princes, Politics, and Religion, 1547–1589*. London: Hambledon Press, 1984.

Turchetti, Mario. "Religious Concord and Political Tolerance in Sixteenth- and Seventeenth-Century France." *Sixteenth Century Journal* 22, no. 1 (1991): 15–25.

Wolfe, Michael. *The Conversion of Henri IV: Politics, Power, and Religious Belief in Early Modern France*. Cambridge, Mass.: Harvard University Press, 1993.

Wood, James B. *The King's Army: Warfare, Soldiers, and Society during the Wars of Religion in France, 1562–1572*. Cambridge: Cambridge University Press, 1996.

THE SAINT BARTHOLOMEW'S DAY MASSACRE
IN LITERATURE AND THE ARTS

Chénier, Marie-Joseph. *Charles IX, ou l'école des rois*. 1788. Drama.

Chéreau, Patrice. *Queen Margot*. 1994. Film.

D'Aubigné, Agrippa. *Les tragiques*. 1616. Epic poem.

Dumas, Alexandre. *Marguerite de Valois*. 1845. Novel.

Griffith, D. W. *Intolerance*. 1916. Film.

Marlowe, Christopher. *The Massacre at Paris*. 1593. Drama.

Meyerbeer, Giacomo. *Les Huguenots*. 1836. Opera.

Acknowledgments (continued from p. iv)

Introduction: Portions of this introduction have appeared in Barbara B. Diefendorf, "Memories of the Massacre: Saint Bartholomew's Day and Protestant Identity in France," in *Voices for Tolerance in an Age of Persecution*, edited by Vincent P. Carey with Ronald Bogdan and Elizabeth Walsh, pp. 45–63. Washington, D.C.: Folger Shakespeare Library, 2004.

Document 16: Excerpt from pp. 232–39 from *The Pursuit of Power: Venetian Ambassadors' Reports*, Edited and Translated by James C. Davis. English translation copyright © 1970 by James C. Davis. Reprinted by permission of HarperCollins Publishers.

Document 36: From Michel de Montaigne, translated by Donald M. Frame. *The Complete Works of Montaigne, Essays, Travel Journals, Letters.* Copyright © 1943 by Donald M. Frame, renewed 1971; © 1948, 1957, 1958 by the Board of Trustees of the Leland Stanford Junior University. All rights reserved. Used with the permission of Stanford University Press, www.sup.org.

Document 37: Courtesy of Peter Gay.

Document 38: Courtesy of the Féderation Protestante de France.

Document 39: © Libreria Editrice Vaticana, 2007.

Index